COASTAL CAROLINA COOKIN

DATE DUE

			PRINTED IN U.S.A.

Coastal Carolina Cooking

NANCY DAVIS & KATHY HART

Illustrations by Deborah Haeffele

The University of North Carolina Press

Chapel Hill & London

Copyright © 1986 The University of North Carolina Press

Manufactured in the United States of America

Library of Congress Cataloging-in-Publication Data

Davis, Nancy, 1960–

Coastal Carolina cooking.

Includes index.

1. Cookery—North Carolina.   I. Hart, Kathy,

1957–   . II. Title.

TX715.D26518   1986   641.59756′1   85-22265

ISBN 0-8078-1692-2

ISBN 0-8078-4152-8 (pbk.)

98   7 6 5 4

To
Dot and G. C. Davis,
Bert and Gene Hart,
Philip Safriet, and
Jessie Sharpe

CONTENTS

Frances Drane **Inglis** Edenton 35	*Baked shad, rock muddle, fried herring roe, baked shad roe, fish pie, roasted goose, homemade catsup, tomato sauce, corn dodgers, egg bread, beaten biscuits, artichoke pickles, lemon chess pie, apple crisp, Blight House plum pudding*
Jeanie Williams Manteo 47	*Roasted swan, clam chowder with rice, bluefish cakes, mashed rutabagas, mashed turnips, stewed tomatoes, string beans with potatoes and cornmeal dumplings, yeast rolls, sticky buns, chocolate pound cake*
Nora **Scarborough** Wanchese 54	*Crab soup, crab cakes, fresh tuna fish salad, raw oysters, stewed shrimp, oyster dressing for turkey*
Lucille Osborne Engelhard 58	*Baked country ham, fried pork chops, chicken soup with vegetables, mashed potatoes, baked tomatoes, lacy corn bread, raw apple cake, pineapple upside-down cake*
Sarah Latham Belhaven 64	*Fried butterfish, baked sugar-cured ham, fried chicken, baked chicken dressing, ham rolls, blueberry cake, fruit salad, molasses pie, pull candy, drop doughnuts, brown sugar chewy cake, fudge*
Venice Williams Avon 72	*Fried spot, stewed pork chops and pork liver with dumplings and pastry, fried chicken, corn pone bread, coconut pie, blackberry spread*

Evelyn Styron Hatteras 76	*Fried trout, broiled trout, stewed goose, potato salad, cole slaw, fig pudding, pumpkin pie*
Elizabeth Howard Ocracoke 81	*Puppy drum and potatoes, baked leg of lamb, blackberry or apple dumplings, jelly cake, chocolate cake*
Lucille Truitt Oriental 87	*Old drum stew, fried mullet, broiled Spanish mackerel, venison ham, collards and Irish potatoes, chocolate cake*
Glennie Willis Atlantic 91	*Fried scallops, stewed oysters, deviled crab casserole, fish hash, spot and sweet potatoes, stewed diamondback terrapin, stewed venison, stewed rutabagas*
Mitchell and **Vilma Morris** Smyrna 98	*Stew-fried shrimp, oyster stew, oyster fritters, stew-fried birds, molasses gunger*
Bill and **Eloise Pigott** Gloucester 103	*Conch chowder, cornmeal dumplings, Downeast clam bake, clam fritters, hard crab stew, crab cakes, pecan pie*
Georgie Bell **Nelson** Harkers Island 109	*Clam chowder with cornmeal dumplings, collards with cornmeal dumplings, stew-fried corn, fried sweet potatoes, fig preserves, coconut pie, bread pudding*

Jessie Savage Morehead City 115	*Conch stew, cornmeal dumplings, fried hogfish, shad roe with sweet potatoes, sea mullet stew, cabbage, hush puppies*
Rita Guthrie and Flora Bell Pittman Salter Path 120	*Baked bluefish, stewed pompano, spareribs and rutabagas, fried mullet roe, stewed chicken, mullet and watermelon, scallop fritters, lightning rolls, stovetop corn bread, rice custard*
Letha Henderson Hubert 126	*Liver pudding, sausage, souse, hog brains and eggs, stone crab cakes, boiled shrimp, coon hash, grape pie, applejacks or peachjacks, pound cake, yaupon tea, sassafras tea*
Flonnie Hood and Dorothy Hood Mills Burgaw 136	*Chicken and pastry, squirrel and dumplings, fried squirrel, pig tails and rice, deviled crabs, baked shad, shad roe and eggs, red-eye gravy, grits, rice, cream-style corn, butter beans, fried okra, baked corn bread, biscuits, pecan pie, cold-oven pound cake*
Percy Jenkins and Loraine Jenkins Sneads Ferry 146	*Fried shrimp, fish stew, crab soup, oyster stew, hush puppies, fried scallops, fried soft-shell crabs, baked fish with crab meat, stewed mullet with sweet potatoes and cornmeal dumplings, blueberry dumplings*
Sunshyne Davis and Jo Ann Davis Griffin Wilmington and Holden Beach 152	*Duck and wild rice casserole, sautéed shrimp, steamed oysters, red snapper throats, fish cakes, venison stew, venison meat loaf, frog legs, bear roast, stuffed tomatoes, fried sweet potatoes, cheese-onion bread, sweet potato pie, lemon meringue pie*

ACKNOWLEDGMENTS

We would like to thank the following people for their help in compiling this book: Joyce Taylor, seafood agent with the University of North Carolina Sea Grant College Program, for sharing her knowledge about seafood; B. J. Copeland, director of the Sea Grant Program, for allowing us to pursue this project; Jim Bahen, Bob Hines, and Randy Rouse, marine advisory agents with the Sea Grant Program, and Rhett White, director of the North Carolina Marine Resources Center on Roanoke Island, for supplying the names of several cooks; the North Carolina Agricultural Extension Service home extension agents in many coastal counties who supplied us with more names of coastal cooks; Carolyn Lackey and Nadine Tope of the North Carolina Agricultural Extension Service for assistance with many of the pickling and preserving recipes; and Dorothy Davis and Bert Hart, for their comments and support.

Foremost, we would like to thank those who are included in these pages. They opened their homes, reached into their recipe boxes and drawers, dusted off their memories, and talked to us about food and recipes.

INTRODUCTION

This is a book about the traditional cooks and cooking of the North Carolina coast. In its pages, you will meet thirty-four cooks from Currituck County to Brunswick County and everywhere in between who have shared dishes you do not find on restaurant menus or in the pages of fancy cookbooks. The recipes start with the basics and almost never call for a can of soup or a ready-made pie crust.

To hear cooks like Eloise Pigott of Gloucester and Letha Henderson of Hubert tell it, you would think there was nothing special about their ways of cooking. They can hardly believe you are asking about their recipes—ones that were passed along from a relative or neighbor and are as much a part of coastal tradition as boatbuilding and netmaking. But we did ask, and the cooks shared more than just their recipes. They told us about their families, their traditions, their way of life—all in the context of food.

Food is central to the family in coastal North Carolina, and it is associated with togetherness and good times. The aromas of frying bacon or a simmering stew signaled the beginning and end of each day when all the family gathered at the table.

Sometimes, food drew together more than just the family. Clam bakes, oyster roasts, and mullet barbecues were gatherings for the whole community. At these events, tables were laden with each cook's best efforts. Food also drew together the young; many a girl's first date was a fudge party or candy pull supervised by her mother.

As anywhere, food had its seasonal aspects too. People ate seafoods, meats, wild game, vegetables, and fruits according to the season. When possible, they extended the availability of these seasonal foods by corning, smoking, salting, canning and preserving, and pickling.

To find those who knew how to corn fish and salt pork, we called home economics extension agents and Sea Grant marine advisory agents in the coastal counties. We explained that we were looking for good cooks from long-time coastal families. They provided us with names of cooks or the names of those who would know good cooks. Then we set out to meet these people in person. A few were hesitant at first, but we found that if there is one topic that will open up a conversation, it's food. It seems that if people enjoy cooking and eating good food, they enjoy talking about it.

We had one problem. Most of the cooks measured their ingredients by the handful or the pinch. When we asked them how much water to add to a cornmeal dumpling, they were likely to answer, "Just enough." Measuring cups and spoons were as foreign to these people as cake mixes and artificial flavorings. But we pushed and prodded and tested their memories. Finally, we learned that "just enough" was four tablespoons, not two or three.

Some of our cooks treated us to a taste of their cooking. Others, like the Morrises in Smyrna, prepared a feast of seafoods with all the fixings. In Edenton, Frances Inglis pulled out a handwritten family cookbook compiled in the 1860s. And Katherine Taylor in Maple still refers to a 1924 cookbook that she used in her high school home economics class.

Most of the cooks we included grew up in families that combined farming and fishing. For the most part, they were self-sufficient. If they went to the grocery store, it was for flour, sugar, and coffee or tea. Often, it wasn't money that changed hands for these goods; the storekeeper would accept a few dozen eggs in return.

Although many of the cooks' families were not wealthy by today's standards, they were rich in the variety of foods that blessed their table. They knew

the goodness of fresh seafood, just-picked vegetables, and freshly churned butter. They cooked these
ingredients into dishes that pleased the palate and
nourished the body.

When we set out to compile this book, we thought
we would find distinct regional differences in the
cooking. Instead, we discovered that a cook from
Manteo is just as likely to drop cornmeal dumplings
into her collards as are cooks from Downeast towns
like Gloucester and Atlantic. We did find that, from
north to south, cooks used species of fish according
to their availability. Dishes using herring and striped
bass were prevalent in the north, drum along the
Outer Banks, and catfish in the south.

With a few exceptions, most of the cooks we interviewed were men and women old enough to remember when shrimp were a dime a bucket and soft-shell
crabs were just coastal fare. They know how to slice
a freshly killed hog into more than ham and bacon;
from head to tail, they used every ounce of meat and
fat.

These are special people, and they are what make
this book more than a compilation of recipes. It's a
taste of home.

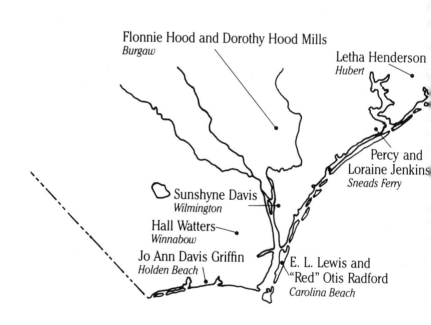

Flonnie Hood and Dorothy Hood Mills
Burgaw

Letha Henderson
Hubert

Percy and
Loraine Jenkins
Sneads Ferry

Sunshyne Davis
Wilmington

Hall Watters
Winnabow

Jo Ann Davis Griffin
Holden Beach

E. L. Lewis and
"Red" Otis Radford
Carolina Beach

Katherine and Emest Taylor
Maple

Jemima Markham
Elizabeth City

Mae Tarkington
Camden

Dorothy Treadwell
Grandy

Vera Gallop
Harbinger

Jeanie Williams
Manteo

Nora Scarborough
Wanchese

Frances Drane Inglis
Edenton

Sarah Latham
Belhaven

Lucille Osborne
Engelhard

Venice Williams
Avon

Evelyn Styron
Hatteras

Lucille Truitt
Oriental

Elizabeth Howard
Ocracoke

Glennie Willis
Atlantic

ie Savage
head City

Mitchell and Vilma Morris
Smyrna

Bill and Eloise Pigott
Gloucester

Georgie Bell Nelson
Harkers Island

Rita Guthrie and Flora Bell Pittman
Salter Path

COASTAL CAROLINA COOKING

KATHERINE & EMEST TAYLOR
Maple

C oons to coots, bass to bluefish, Katherine Taylor has put them all on the table. Born not long after the turn of the century, Katherine and her husband, Emest, learned early that wild or tame, cultivated or free-growing, nothing was allowed to go to waste. With the proper seasonings and preparation, even the wildest game and the tartest fruit could tempt the taste buds.

On Katherine's homestead in Shawboro, her parents raised "a little of everything"—fruits, vegetables, geese, turkeys, guineas, goats, chickens, sheep, and hogs. In those days, the kitchen was separated from the house. Katherine's mother would cook up the farm's bounty on a wood stove. Then the meal was carried to the main house. This arrangement confined the odors and the heat from cooking in an outbuilding and reduced the danger of house fires.

When it came time for Katherine to begin cooking for her own family, she used many of her mother's recipes. If she had a question about measurements, she referred to the cookbook she was issued in her home economics class in 1924.

A native of Maple, eighty-five-year-old Emest remembers fishing for redfin perch along marsh roads trafficked with horses and buggies. And he recalls the days when a man's farm was sized as "one-horse or two-horse."

For fifty-four years, Emest was the flour-and-sugar of Maple. He ran the community's general merchandise, where he sold sugar, lard, and pickled pork, packaged not in plastic, but in large barrels.

BAKED BASS

Katherine recommends skinning a largemouth bass. "The skin is tough and has a musty flavor," she says.

1 4-pound largemouth bass, dressed
½ teaspoon salt
2 onions, sliced
3 Irish potatoes, sliced
8 bacon strips

Place bass in a roasting pan. Salt. Layer onions and potatoes over the fish. Top with bacon strips. Bake in a 350-degree oven 30 to 40 minutes. Serves 4.

BAKED BLUEFISH IN A BAG

The bag, says Katherine, keeps the oily bluefish from popping and retains more of the fish's moisture.

4 small bluefish (about 1 pound each), dressed
1 teaspoon salt
½ teaspoon black pepper
4 paper bags

Season bluefish with salt and pepper. Place each fish in a paper bag and twist the bag shut. Place on a baking sheet in a 275-degree oven. Bake 30 minutes or until the fish flakes. Serves 4.

FRIED WHITE PERCH

8 to 10 perch fillets
1 cup white cornmeal
2 teaspoons salt
1 teaspoon black pepper
½ cup vegetable oil or shortening

Roll the fillets in cornmeal. Salt and pepper. Fry in oil or shortening in an iron skillet over medium high heat. Serves 4.

FRESHNESS

With seafood, freshness is essential; mishandled fish can ruin a good recipe. At the seafood market and in the grocery store, consumers can test the freshness of fish for themselves by using the following indicators:

• A fresh fish has an odor that is fresh and mild, as though it had just been pulled from the water. A "fishy" smell denotes mishandling.

• The eyes of a fresh fish are bright, clear, full, and often protruding. As a fish deteriorates, its eyes become cloudy, pink, and sunken.

• The gills should be bright red or pink, and free from slime.

• The intestinal cavity should be pink, with a bright red blood streak. The streak should not be brown.

• The skin of a fresh fish is shiny and not faded, with scales that adhere tightly. Its flesh is firm and elastic and springs back when pressed gently with the finger. As a fish ages, its flesh becomes soft and slimy, and slips away from the bone.

Note: This information was provided by Joyce Taylor, UNC Sea Grant's seafood specialist at the North Carolina State University Seafood Laboratory in Morehead City.

FRIED OYSTERS

1 large egg
3 tablespoons milk
1 pint oysters
¾ cup cornmeal
1 teaspoon salt
½ teaspoon black pepper
½ cup vegetable oil or shortening

In a mixing bowl, beat together egg and milk. Dip oysters one by one into egg mixture. Dredge oysters in cornmeal that has been seasoned with salt and pepper. Panfry in oil or shortening in a skillet over medium high heat until golden brown. Serves 4.

FRIED HERRING

4 ¾-pound corned herring, dressed
1 cup cornmeal
6 tablespoons vegetable oil or shortening

Remove herring from its salty preservative. Soak for 6 to 8 hours in fresh water in the refrigerator to remove the salt. Dredge in cornmeal. Panfry in oil or shortening in a skillet over medium high heat until very crisp. Serves 4.

FRIED COOT

1 coot, plucked, skinned, and cleaned
¾ cup plain flour
1 teaspoon salt
½ teaspoon black pepper
¼ cup shortening or vegetable oil

Cut up coot as you would a chicken. Combine flour, salt, and pepper in a mixing bowl. Dredge coot in flour. Panfry in hot shortening or oil in large skillet, browning all sides. Serves 4.

FRIED RABBIT

1 3- to 4-pound rabbit, headed, cleaned, skinned,
   and cut into serving pieces
½ cup plain flour
2 teaspoons salt
1 teaspoon black pepper
1 cup vegetable oil or shortening

Dust the rabbit pieces with flour. Salt and pepper. Panfry in oil or shortening in a skillet over medium heat until golden brown. If the rabbit is not parboiled, reduce heat and cook until the juices run clear when the meat is pierced. Serves 2.

ROASTED COON

1 raccoon, headed, gutted, and skinned
water
1 to 2 pods dried hot pepper
2 teaspoons salt
2 to 3 tablespoons dried sage

Remove the scent glands from under the front legs and each thigh of the coon. Place the coon in a large saucepan; cover with water. Add salt and pepper pods. Parboil until meat is tender. Remove and place in a roasting pan. Rub coon with sage. Roast in a 350-degree oven for 1 hour. Serves 4.

MAY PEAS

2 cups shelled peas
1½ quarts water
½ teaspoon salt
small piece of ham or a thin slice of salt pork
8 to 10 small new potatoes

Add peas, water, salt, ham or salt pork, and potatoes to a medium saucepan. Bring to a boil. Reduce heat and simmer 20 minutes. Serves 4.

WATERMELON RIND PICKLES

8 cups watermelon rind
½ cup salt
1½ quarts cold water
4 cups sugar

2 cups vinegar
3 sticks cinnamon
15 to 18 whole cloves
15 to 19 whole allspice
piece of cheesecloth, 6 × 6 inches
string
sterilized quart jars

Remove the pink pulp and outer dark green rind of
the watermelon. Cut remaining green pulp into small
chunks (1 inch × 1 inch). Place in a large bowl. Mix
salt with 1½ quarts cold water. Pour over rind and
soak for 6 hours or overnight. Drain, rinse, and cover
rind with cold water. In a large saucepan, cook rind
in water until it is tender. Drain well. Combine sugar
and vinegar. Tie spices in cheesecloth. Add to vinegar and sugar. Bring to a boil and add rind. Reduce
heat and simmer until rind is clear. Remove spice
bag. Pack rinds into hot, sterilized jars. Cover rinds
with boiling liquid, leaving a 1-inch air space at the
top. Seal and process 15 minutes in a boiling-water
bath. Makes 2 to 3 quarts.

This recipe has been in Katherine's family "for-ever and ever."

BANANA CAKE

1 cup butter, room temperature
2 cups sugar
4 eggs, room temperature
1 teaspoon vanilla
3 cups sifted plain flour
2 teaspoons baking powder
¼ teaspoon salt
1 cup milk or water, room temperature
4 medium bananas, ripe
icing (see recipe below)

Cream butter and sugar. Add eggs one at a time,
beating after each. Add vanilla. Beat batter until
fluffy. Sift together flour, baking powder, and salt. Alternately add flour and milk or water to batter. Mix at

low speed. Pour batter into 4 8-inch layer-cake pans, greased and lined with waxed paper. Bake at 375 degrees until the centers spring back, about 25 to 30 minutes.

To assemble, spread a thin coating of icing on bottom layer of cake. Top with thin slices of banana. Spread more icing on top of bananas. Continue with other layers, adding icing and bananas each time. Cover sides and top layer with icing.

Butter icing
1½ sticks butter or margarine, softened
1½ boxes confectioners sugar
2 to 4 teaspoons water

Cream together butter and sugar. Add water until icing becomes smooth and creamy.

DOROTHY TREADWELL
Grandy

Dorothy Treadwell proudly identifies herself as one of the "mighty Midgetts" of North Carolina's Outer Banks. Synonymous with the Midgett family name is the tradition of waterfowl hunting. Dorothy's father, Harrison Midgett, was born in Chicamacomico, now Rodanthe, in 1889, but he moved north to Currituck, where he was a sharecrop farmer by trade and a professional hunting and fishing guide at heart.

"My father could call in the ducks and geese like no other," says Dorothy. Using his mouth to imitate their calls, Harrison clucked at ducks and honked at geese. Those were the "market days," when hunters came from all over to cash in on the abundant waterfowl and shipped them out to northern markets, literally, by the barrel. It was not uncommon for a hunter to kill hundreds of ducks and geese in a day. As word of the waterfowl lode spread northward during the late 1800s, the wealthy of New York and Boston came to isolated Currituck County to see for themselves. More often than not, they wanted a "local" to supply the hunting expertise. And like many others, Dorothy's father guided his share of the rich and famous through the grasses of Currituck Sound.

What does Dorothy remember most about those days with her father? "The good food and good fellowship that went along with the waterfowl tradition."

Dorothy says she is not a hunter herself, but she knows how to cook the catch. She started working in a restaurant when she was nineteen. Since then, she has managed restaurants, school and hospital cafeterias, and snack bars. Those may be places where there aren't many chances to serve a baked wild goose, but she hasn't forgotten how.

BAKED WILD GOOSE

Dorothy places an apple, potato, or rutabaga inside the goose to absorb some of the wild, fishy flavor of the bird.

1 dressed wild goose
1 teaspoon salt
1 teaspoon black pepper
1 teaspoon sage
1 apple, potato, or rutabaga
4 cups water
1 bay leaf
cheesecloth to cover bird

Wash and clean fowl. Rub salt on outside skin and pepper and sage inside the cavity. Place the fruit or vegetable inside the fowl and place fowl in a large roasting pan. Add water and bay leaf. Bake at 350 degrees for 4 hours. More water may be needed as fowl cooks. When tender, remove fowl from pan. Pour off excess juices and save. Return fowl to pan and cover with clean cheesecloth soaked in the excess juices. Turn up oven to 425 degrees and brown fowl with cloth on top. Remove vegetable before serving and discard. Serves 6 to 8.

CRAB MEAT CASSEROLE

2 eggs, beaten
1 cup mayonnaise
1 cup milk
1 teaspoon seafood seasoning
¼ teaspoon dried red pepper
¼ teaspoon salt
1 4-ounce jar minced pimento
½ cup chopped green pepper
1 pound cooked crab meat
1 cup white bread, edged and diced

In a large mixing bowl, combine eggs, mayonnaise, milk, and seasonings. Add pimento, green pepper, and crab. Stir in bread. Spread in an 8 × 12-inch buttered pan and bake at 350 degrees for 45 minutes. When casserole is done, a knife inserted in center should come out clean. Serves 4 to 6.

FRIED SWEET POTATOES

1 stick butter or margarine
4 medium sweet potatoes, peeled and sliced
1 cup sugar
½ to 1 teaspoon cinnamon
1 cup water

In a large skillet, melt butter. Add remaining ingredients and cover. Simmer until potatoes are tender. Remove lid and continue to simmer until water cooks out and potatoes become brown. Serves 4.

SOUPY GREEN BEANS AND POTATOES

Dorothy likes to eat her beans and potatoes like soup in a bowl. Her favorite side dishes include corn bread and a sweet potato.

2 slices salt pork
4 cups water
3 cups snapped green beans
2 medium Irish potatoes, diced

Place salt pork in a large saucepan. Add water and bring to a boil. Add beans and potatoes. Reduce heat and simmer for 1 hour. Serves 4.

MASHED RUTABAGA

When Dorothy has leftover mashed rutabaga, she likes to fry it in patties. She advises making extra so you will have plenty of leftovers.

1 rutabaga, peeled and sliced
water
1 teaspoon salt
2 tablespoons butter

BLUE CRAB

The blue crab has some of the sweetest meat the ocean has to offer. But unfortunately, the crab has a rather nasty disposition. If not handled carefully, the crab can make an unforgettable impression with its sharp claws.

Commercial fishermen capture these fighting crustaceans with pots, nets, and dredges. The recreational crabber is more likely to use a dip net, a baited string, or a pot.

Walking the estuarine shoreline with a dip net can yield the recreational crabber a fair number of these blue-green crustaceans. But baiting a string or a pot will present a more attractive lure and better chances for a full cooking pot.

To use a bait line, tie a chicken neck or fish head to the end of a string. Slowly lower it into the water. When a crab begins nibbling at the bait, slowly raise the line to the surface and carefully slip the dip net under him.

The crab pot, which is easy to build, can trap ten to twelve crabs in several hours during warm weather. Best of all, it does not need tending. Built of wire mesh and baited with fish heads or fish remains, the trap is designed to allow an easy entrance but a difficult escape for the crab.

Once the crab is on dry land, it should be kept alive until it is placed in the cooking pot. Place your catch in a tub, basket, or box, cover with a moistened burlap bag, and keep in a cool place until ready for cooking.

In a large saucepan, boil rutabaga until tender in water seasoned with salt. Remove from water, add butter, and mash with a potato masher or fork. Serves 2.

Dorothy says this relish is delicious on meats, seafood, and vegetables.

BELL PEPPER RELISH

1 dozen green bell peppers
1 dozen red bell peppers
water
1 quart vinegar
1 small can whole pickling spices
piece of cheesecloth, 6 × 6 inches
string
4 cups sugar
sterilized pint jars

Wash and core peppers. Grind peppers in a meat chopper. Place in a large saucepan and cover with water. Boil for 5 minutes. Remove from stove. Drain peppers and set aside. In a saucepan, combine vinegar and 1 quart water. Tie pickling spices into a piece of cheesecloth. Add to water and vinegar. Add sugar and bring mixture to a boil. Reduce heat. Add drained peppers and simmer 10 minutes. Remove from stove for 1 hour. Reheat and simmer 10 more minutes. Place relish in sterile jars, leaving a ½-inch air space at the top. Seal jars and process in a boiling-water bath for 10 minutes. Makes about 6 pints.

Dorothy uses the figs as a side relish dish. Although she leaves her figs unpeeled, home economists suggest peeling the fruit.

PICKLED FIGS

3 quarts figs
1 tablespoon whole cloves
1 bay leaf
1 tablespoon allspice
1 piece of cheesecloth, 6 × 6 inches
kitchen string
1 cup vinegar
6 cups sugar
sterilized pint jars

Wash figs and peel. If unpeeled figs are preferred, pour boiling water over them and let stand until

14

cool; drain. Tie spices in a cheesecloth bag. Add to vinegar and sugar in a large saucepan. Bring to a boil. Add figs and reduce heat. Simmer for 10 minutes. Remove from stove, cover, and set aside. The next day, bring figs and syrup to a boil, reduce heat, and simmer 10 minutes. Cover and set aside. On third day, repeat process. Place figs and syrup in hot sterilized jars, leaving a ½-inch air space at the top. Seal jars and process in a boiling-water bath for 10 minutes. Makes 6 pints.

MAE TARKINGTON
Camden

Mae Tarkington grew up on a farm in the Possum Quarter community of Pasquotank County. "My daddy raised most everything we ate. He even grew his own cane for making molasses," says Mae.

For meat, her family raised hogs and chickens. And they bartered the chicken eggs for the few groceries they bought at a nearby market. "Once a week, the fish man came around in an old truck and we bought fish from him," says Mae.

To preserve the hog meat, Mae's father smoked the hams, shoulders, and sausage and salted the sides and head in a wooden barrel, alternating layers of meat with layers of salt. When her mother removed the meat from the barrel, a piece at a time, she used it for flavoring vegetables, especially greens. Mae's favorite was the meat of the hog's head. "It's real sweet," she says.

After a hog killing, Mae's mother rendered the fat from the hogs for lard, which she flavored with bay. The crisp remains of the meat left after the rendering were called "cracklings." Her mother dropped the cracklings in corn bread, biscuits, and hominy for added flavor.

For milk, butter, and clabber, the family kept a cow. One of Mae's favorites for breakfast was clabber and molasses in a bowl.

Since her younger years in Possum Quarter, Mae has moved down the road to Camden, where she has the reputation of being the best cook of corn bread and biscuits in the county. When her son was young, many of his friends hung around until mealtime just to get a slice of Mae's sweet, moist corn bread. The secret, she says, is using white cornmeal and just the right amount of sugar. "Too much sugar will make it stick," she says.

CORN BREAD

1 cup medium-ground white cornmeal
1 cup plain flour
2 cups milk
1 egg
⅓ cup sugar
1 teaspoon salt
1 stick margarine

In a mixing bowl, combine cornmeal and flour. Stir in 1½ cups of milk, egg, sugar, and salt. Melt margarine in baking pan. Pour margarine into cornmeal mixture and set baking pan aside. Add remaining milk, and mix. Pour batter into an 8 × 10-inch baking pan (the melted butter has greased it). Bake in a 400-degree oven until brown.

GRIDDLE CAKES

Using corn bread recipe, fry batter like pancakes. Drop batter by the spoonful onto a hot greased griddle. Mae says two or three spoonfuls of batter will make a nice cake. Fry until brown on both sides. Serve as bread for lunch or supper.

VEGETABLE SOUP

1½ to 2 pounds soup beef
1 quart water
1½ cups corn
1½ cups green peas
1½ cups butter beans
16 ounces canned tomatoes
4 carrots, diced
1 small onion, diced
1 can tomato soup

For her vegetable soup, Mae uses the shank portion of beef. She cooks the beef a day ahead of time and places the beef and stock in the refrigerator overnight. She says this recipe makes enough for several meals, so she freezes the leftovers.

17

Place beef in a large roasting pan. Add water. Roast for 1 hour at 325 degrees. Store beef and stock overnight in the refrigerator. The next day, skim fat from the top of stock and discard, retaining stock. Pull meat from the bone and chop meat into bite-size pieces. Place in a large saucepan and add beef stock. Add vegetables, tomato soup, and more water if needed. Stew for 1 hour.

BUTTERMILK YEAST BISCUITS

Instead of baking all sixty biscuits at once, Mae freezes some of the uncooked biscuits on cookie sheets lined with wax paper. When they are frozen, she stores them in plastic bags.

5 cups plain flour
5 teaspoons baking powder
1 teaspoon salt
½ teaspoon baking soda
3 tablespoons sugar
1 cup shortening
2 cups buttermilk
1 package yeast dissolved in 5 tablespoons
    lukewarm water

In a large mixing bowl, sift together flour, baking powder, salt, baking soda, and sugar. Cut in shortening. Stir in buttermilk. Add yeast mixture. Knead lightly. Roll dough onto a floured surface using a rolling pin. Cut with biscuit cutter. Bake on greased baking sheet 10 to 12 minutes at 450 degrees. Makes 60 biscuits.

NEVER-FAIL PAN ROLLS

Mae says this dough will keep in the refrigerator for a week.

¾ cup sugar
¾ cup shortening
1 cup boiling water
2 packages dry yeast
1 cup warm water
2 eggs, slightly beaten
6 to 7 cups plain flour

FLOUR

After the Civil War, the flour milling industry achieved mass production and biscuits became a larger part of the southern diet. To make biscuits, cooks combined plain flour with baking powder or soda, sweet or sour milk (sometimes buttermilk), hog lard, and a pinch of salt. By varying the amounts of these ingredients, cooks baked flat or fluffy biscuits that were eaten from breakfast to dinner.

1 teaspoon salt
1 teaspoon baking powder
½ teaspoon baking soda

In a large mixing bowl, cream sugar and shortening until light and fluffy. Add boiling water. Mix thoroughly and let cool. In a small mixing bowl, dissolve yeast in warm water and set aside. Add eggs to cooled shortening mixture and mix well. Stir in yeast mixture. Combine 5 cups flour with salt, baking powder, and soda. Add to yeast mixture and mix well. Turn out dough on well-floured surface. Knead in enough remaining flour until dough is no longer sticky. Roll into 1½-inch balls. Place balls, nearly touching, in greased 9-inch round cake pans. Cover and let rolls rise in warm place until doubled. Bake at 400 degrees for 20 minutes. Makes 3 dozen.

CUCUMBER RELISH

Mae uses her relish over chicken and in potato salad.

¼ cup salt
13 cups cucumbers, finely chopped
cold water
ice cubes

3½ cups sugar
2 cups white vinegar
1 tablespoon celery seed
1 tablespoon mustard seed
½ teaspoon turmeric
5 to 6 sterilized pint jars

In a large mixing bowl, sprinkle salt over cucumbers and cover with cold water and ice cubes. Let stand for 4 hours. Drain in a colander and press out as much liquid as possible. In a large saucepan, mix sugar, vinegar, celery seed, mustard seed, and turmeric. Bring to a boil. When sugar is dissolved, stir in cucumbers. Reduce heat and simmer 10 minutes. Pack hot into sterilized jars. Process jars in a boiling-water bath for 10 minutes.

COCA-COLA CAKE

2 cups plain flour
2 cups sugar
3 tablespoons cocoa
2 sticks butter or margarine
1 cup Coca-Cola
½ cup buttermilk
2 eggs, beaten
1 teaspoon baking soda
1 teaspoon vanilla
2 cups miniature marshmallows
icing (see recipe below)

In a large mixing bowl, combine flour and sugar. In a medium saucepan, combine cocoa, butter, and Coca-Cola. Bring to a boil and remove from heat. Add sugar and flour and mix well. Add buttermilk, eggs, baking soda, and vanilla. Mix well. Stir in marshmallows. Bake in a 9 × 12-inch pan at 350 degrees for 40 minutes. Cool and top with icing.

Icing

1 stick butter or margarine
3 tablespoons cocoa
6 tablespoons Coca-Cola
1 box powdered sugar
1 cup pecans, chopped

In a medium saucepan, melt butter or margarine.
Add remaining ingredients and mix well.

JEMIMA MARKHAM
Elizabeth City

Jemima James Markham's favorite childhood breakfast was rich. But who can fault a girl for enjoying the goodness of fresh thick cream poured over just-picked strawberries and accompanied by hot biscuits and freshly churned butter? Most of the ingredients for this meal and every other meal set upon the James's table came from the fertile lowland that surrounded their home.

Jemima and her nine brothers and sisters were reared in Weeksville, a town on the edge of Pasquotank River. Her father farmed and fished. The result of his endeavors—fruits, vegetables, meats, fish, grains, and dairy products—met virtually all of the family's nutritional needs. Her mother took these homegrown products and made them into simple, wholesome meals.

"Our mother was a wonderful cook, very creative," Jemima says. "But she used a pinch of this and a dash of that without definite recipes. She taught us the joy of eating well-balanced meals with emphasis on vegetables and fruits, raw as well as cooked.

"Leafy and root vegetables were always available and often cooked together," Jemima says. "Of course they were cooked within hours of being gathered. Oh, that taste of freshness."

For those items fishing and farming could not provide, the Jameses traveled by boat to Elizabeth City. They bought flour by the barrel, sharp cheddar cheese by the round, and navy beans and sugar in 100-pound bags. "The ice man came once a week," Jemima says. "He brought a 300-pound cake of ice for the ice box. We placed our pans of milk over it to keep them cool."

Many of the family's social activities had food as their focal point. When the James daughters began to attract suitors, their social activities, or "dates," usually centered around stirring up fudge, mixing together molasses popcorn, or stretching out pull candy. Jemima calls this "wise guidance" on the part of her mother.

CORN PUDDING

If using fresh corn, cut corn from the cob, then scrape cobs to remove all juices, Jemima says. The secret to this dish, she proclaims, is the slow cooking.

¼ cup margarine
2 large eggs
¾ cup milk
¼ cup sugar
3 tablespoons plain flour
¼ teaspoon salt
2 cups corn, fresh or frozen

Melt margarine in a 1½-quart casserole. In a mixing bowl, beat eggs until fluffy. Add milk, melted margarine, sugar, flour, and salt. Stir. Fold in corn. Pour into buttered casserole. Bake for 45 minutes in a 300-degree oven. Serves 4.

STEWED CORN

1 quart fresh-cut corn
1 cup water
3 tablespoons butter or margarine
¼ cup sugar
1 teaspoon salt

In a large saucepan, combine all ingredients. Bring to a boil over medium heat, stirring constantly. Boil 5 to 8 minutes. Serves 8.

CABBAGE SPROUTS

Jemima says that about a week to ten days after cabbage is harvested, small cabbage sprouts appear that resemble brussels sprouts. She says these tender sprouts make an excellent addition to a meal.

20 to 24 cabbage sprouts
2 tablespoons butter
1 teaspoon salt
½ teaspoon black pepper

Using a steamer, steam sprouts until tender (about 5 minutes). Season with butter, salt, and pepper. Serves 4.

PEACH PICKLES

Jemima recommends using June or clingstone peaches. "Don't choose peaches that are over-ripe," she says. She uses the same amounts of sugar, vinegar, and spices for pickling plums.

3 pounds whole peaches, peeled
2 to 4 tablespoons salt
3 cups plus 2 to 4 tablespoons vinegar
3 cups sugar
2 sticks cinnamon
2 tablespoons whole cloves
1 teaspoon whole allspice
piece of cheesecloth, 6 × 6 inches
1 10-inch piece of kitchen string
sterilized quart jars

Wash and peel peaches. Drop peaches into cold water containing 2 tablespoons salt and 2 tablespoons vinegar per gallon of water to prevent browning. Rinse and drain. In a steamer, steam peaches until tender. In a large saucepan, bring sugar and vinegar to a boil. Tie spices in cheesecloth. Add spices to boiling sugar and vinegar. Simmer 20 minutes. Remove spices. Place peaches in hot, sterilized quart jars. Pour boiling syrup over peaches, leaving a 1-inch air space at top. Seal. Process 20 minutes in a boiling-water bath. Yields 2 to 4 quarts.

PICKLED BEETS

Jemima leaves roots and stems on the beets until after she has boiled them. Simply trim the tops, leaving one to two inches of stem. This will help the beets retain their color, she says.

5 pounds whole, small beets, washed
water
3 cups sugar
3 cups vinegar
sterilized pint jars

Place beets in a large saucepan. Cover with water. Bring to a boil, reduce heat, and simmer until beets are tender. (Time will depend on size of beets.) Drain and cool. Trim away roots and stems. Peel and slice. In a saucepan, bring sugar and vinegar to a boil. Add the beets and simmer 10 to 15 minutes. Place beets in hot, sterilized pint jars and pour syrup over, leaving a ½-inch air space at top. Seal. Process in a boiling-water bath for 30 minutes. Yields 4 to 5 pints.

SWEET POTATO BISCUITS

Jemima says these biscuits are a good way of using leftover baked sweet potatoes.

1½ cups sweet potatoes, baked, peeled, and mashed
¾ cup shortening
2 cups plain flour
⅓ cup sugar
2 teaspoons baking powder

In a mixing bowl, add shortening to potatoes while they are still hot. Blend thoroughly. Cool. In another mixing bowl, mix dry ingredients. Add to the sweet potatoes and work dough until blended. Roll out dough on a floured surface to a ½-inch thickness. Cut out biscuits with a biscuit cutter. Place on an ungreased pan. Bake in a 400-degree oven for 12 to 15 minutes or until golden in color. Yields 12 to 16 biscuits.

MOLASSES POPCORN

½ cup popcorn, unpopped
¼ cup vegetable oil
2 cups molasses
1 teaspoon vinegar
3 tablespoons butter

Add popcorn and vegetable oil to a large saucepan.
Place over medium high heat, cover, and pop. Remove popcorn from saucepan, discarding any
unpopped kernels, and place in a large mixing bowl.
Meanwhile, bring molasses to a boil in a saucepan.
Add vinegar. Pour over popcorn. Mix and coat
popcorn thoroughly. Allow to cool slightly. Butter
hands and shape popcorn into balls. Allow to
harden on a buttered cookie sheet.

CHERRY COBBLER

¾ stick margarine
1½ cups sugar
¾ cup self-rising flour
¾ cup milk
2 cups fresh cherries, pitted, or 1 20-ounce can
    pitted sour cherries

Preheat oven to 350 degrees. Melt margarine in a
deep-dish pie pan. In one bowl, mix 1 cup of sugar,
flour, and milk. In another bowl, mix ½ cup sugar
and fruit. Pour batter into pie pan with melted butter.
Add fruit. Do not mix. Bake for 1 hour. Serves 6.

VERA GALLOP
Harbinger

Vera Gallop was reared in the Currituck County community of Point Harbor. In the summer, her father raised fruits and vegetables to sell to the vacationers along Dare County beaches. Vera was rousted from bed at 4:30 in the morning to pick the day's harvest. About mid-morning, her father would head for Dare County with the fresh produce.

"Daddy was particular about the fruits and vegetables he sold," she recalls. "He would never sell a blemished peach or strawberry." Later her father opened a roadside market by his home.

After marrying a fisherman, Vera moved to Harbinger and a house perched on the edge of Currituck Sound. There, she combined her knowledge of fruits and vegetables with a knowledge of fish. During the spring and fall when the fish ran thick, her husband would return to the docks with a mixed load—fifteen boxes (125 to 135 pounds of fish per box) of rockfish, perch, mullet, flounder, or shad. Spring was a time for soft-shell crabs. "Whenever you put the dip net down and pulled it up, you'd have a dip net full of soft crabs."

During the fall mullet runs, Vera's neighbors would assemble for a community treat—a mullet barbecue. The mullet were staked and placed over hot coals. While the mullet cooked, the neighbors enjoyed the fellowship and the view of the sound.

MULLET BARBECUE

charcoal
1 drawn mullet per person
salt and black pepper to taste
1 sharp stick or stake per fish

This dish must be prepared outside over a fire. Using charcoal, build a fire on the ground. Allow the coals to die down. Meanwhile, salt and pepper mullets. Beginning at the mouth, insert a sharp stick or stake (about 2½ feet long) lengthwise through each mullet, leaving the fish at the end of the stick. Insert the bare end of the stick in the ground at a diagonal so that fish extends over the hot coals. Barbecue 20 to 25 minutes.

CRAB SALAD

Vera prefers the backfin meat of the crab rather than claw meat in her salad.

1 pound cooked crab meat
2 boiled eggs, chopped
1 stalk celery, chopped
1 medium onion, chopped
½ cup mayonnaise
1 tablespoon catsup
1 teaspoon salt
½ teaspoon black pepper

In a mixing bowl, combine ingredients. Place on a bed of lettuce or spread on crackers. Serves 4.

FRIED SOFT-SHELL CRABS

1 teaspoon salt
½ teaspoon black pepper
1 cup cornmeal
8 soft-shell crabs, cleaned
½ cup vegetable oil or shortening

In a mixing bowl, combine salt, pepper, and cornmeal. Dredge crabs in cornmeal. Using a large skillet, panfry crabs in oil or shortening over medium heat, browning both sides. Serves 4.

SOFT CRABS

Not too many years ago, soft-shell crabs were only coastal fare. Fishermen received less than a dollar a dozen for them; there was no mention of them on restaurant menus; and inlanders thought they were a separate species of crab. Only recently did land-lubbers learn to eat the soft-shell delicacies, appendages and all.

A soft crab is a hard blue crab that has just shed its shell in preparation for growth. During its three- to four-year lifetime, a blue crab may shed from twenty to thirty times. When it does, the quantity of edible meat exceeds that of a hard crab by ten to fifteen times.

To reap the extra profits that soft crabs offer, fishermen gather crabs that exhibit signs that shedding is imminent. Timing is critical, for during the one to two hours after shedding, the crab absorbs water and completes the expansion of its new shell. It is during that time that the crabs must be har-vested for the soft-shell market. After about four hours, the crab begins to harden unless it is removed from the water. When the shell feels leathery to the touch, the crab has become a "papershell." After about twenty-four hours, the crab's shell becomes hard again.

Coastal cooks advise buying soft crabs alive or frozen. Never buy a soft-shell crab that is dead unless it is frozen. Top-quality crabs should have all their legs and at least one claw.

To clean a soft-shell crab, wash it thoroughly. Turn the crab on its back and lift and remove the apron. Turn the crab over. Lift the large lateral spines of the shell top and scrape away the grayish-white, feathery gills. Remove the eyes and mouth by making one cut just behind the eyes with a knife or kitchen shears. Some cooks advocate removing the top shell completely and scraping away the digestive sac to avoid a sour flavor.

BOILED ROCKFISH

1 5-pound rockfish (striped bass), dressed
water
2 to 3 medium Irish potatoes, diced
1 teaspoon salt
1 teaspoon black pepper
vinegar

Place rockfish in a large saucepan and cover with water. Bring to a boil and reduce heat. Simmer until you can pierce the fish easily with a fork, or 10 minutes per inch of thickness. In another saucepan, cover potatoes with water. Salt and boil until tender. Divide fish into serving portions on plates. Sprinkle with ground pepper and vinegar. Place potatoes on plates. Mash with fork. Serves 6 to 8.

FRIED EELS

2 1- to 1½-pound eels, skinned, cleaned, and boned
¾ cup cornmeal
1 teaspoon salt
½ teaspoon black pepper
½ cup vegetable oil or shortening

Cut eels into 4-inch pieces. In a mixing bowl, combine cornmeal, salt, and pepper. Dredge eel pieces in cornmeal. Using a large skillet, panfry eel in oil or shortening over medium heat, browning both sides. Serves 4.

FRIED SQUASH

1 slice salt pork
3 medium yellow squash (straight neck or
    crooked neck), sliced

1 medium onion, chopped
¼ teaspoon salt

In a medium-sized skillet, render fat from salt pork. Remove meat. Add squash, onions, and salt. Panfry until onions and squash become soft. Serves 4.

FRENCH-FRIED SQUASH

¾ cup plain flour
1 teaspoon salt
½ teaspoon black pepper
3 medium yellow squash (straight neck or
    crooked neck), sliced lengthwise
¾ cup vegetable oil or shortening
salt

In a mixing bowl, combine flour, salt, and pepper. Dredge squash in flour. In a large skillet, panfry in oil or shortening over medium heat, browning both sides. Salt to taste. Serves 4.

SQUASH CAKES

3 yellow squash (straight neck or
    crooked neck), sliced
1 large egg, beaten
1 onion, chopped
¼ cup plain flour
½ cup vegetable oil or shortening

In a medium saucepan, boil squash until tender. Drain. In a mixing bowl, mash squash. Mix in egg, onion, and flour. Drop spoonfuls of mixture into hot oil or shortening in a skillet. Panfry over medium heat, browning both sides. Serves 4.

APPLESAUCE

4 cooking apples, peeled, cored, and sliced
¼ cup water
½ cup sugar
1 teaspoon cinnamon

In a medium saucepan, place sliced apples in water. Boil over medium high heat until apples soften. Mash. Reduce heat to low. Stir in sugar and cinnamon. Serves 4.

SWEET PICKLES

8 pounds small cucumbers, sliced
2 cups pickling lime
8 quarts water
5 pounds sugar
2 quarts vinegar
1 teaspoon salt
2 tablespoons pickling spices
sterilized pint jars

In a large mixing bowl, add cucumbers, lime, and water. Soak overnight. Rinse three times in fresh cool water, then soak 3 more hours in ice water. Drain cucumbers and set aside. Combine sugar, vinegar, salt, and pickling spices. Add cucumbers and let stand 30 minutes. Remove cucumbers and bring syrup and spices to a boil. Reduce heat and simmer 30 minutes. Pack cucumbers into hot, sterilized pint jars. Add hot syrup, leaving a ½-inch air space at the top. Seal and process in a boiling-water bath 20 minutes.

RAISIN PIE

Cover raisins with water and cook five minutes over medium heat. Drain. Vera says this will make raisins plump and more tender.

4 eggs, separated
1 cup sugar
4 tablespoons plain flour
2 cans evaporated milk (13½-ounce cans)
1 15-ounce box raisins
1 teaspoon vanilla
1 9-inch baked pie shell
meringue (see recipe below)

In a mixing bowl, mix egg yolks, sugar, and flour. Gradually add evaporated milk. Place in a double boiler over medium heat. Stirring constantly, cook until thickened. Add raisins and vanilla and pour mixture into a baked pie shell. Cool. Spread meringue over pie, being sure to completely cover filling. Place in a 350-degree oven until meringue browns.

Meringue
4 egg whites
⅓ cup plus 1 tablespoon sugar
¼ teaspoon cream of tartar

In a mixing bowl, beat egg whites with sugar and cream of tartar until stiff.

PEACH COBBLER

1 stick margarine
3 cups peaches, peeled and sliced
¾ cup sugar
½ cup plain flour
½ cup milk

Preheat oven to 350 degrees. In a deep-dish pie pan, melt margarine. In a mixing bowl, coat peaches with

¼ cup of sugar. Mix flour, remaining sugar, and milk. Spread peaches into hot pan with melted margarine. Pour the flour mixture over peaches. Bake 30 to 35 minutes until golden brown.

FRANCES DRANE INGLIS
Edenton

Frances Drane Inglis's home in Edenton is built on a foundation of tradition. The house, called "The Homestead," has stood at the corner of the courthouse green, overlooking Edenton Bay, since 1773. Ships carrying tobacco for England, lumber for the West Indies, naval stores and grain for New England; fishing smacks loaded with herring and shad; watermelon boats; lumber barges; tugs; and now sporty sailing craft have all come within its view. Today Frances raises flowers, herbs, and vegetables in its spacious yard and makes stoneware pottery in the old kitchen building.

Seven generations of Frances's mother's family have occupied its rooms. Her mother restored the two-story, West Indian–style house. It is furnished with family heirlooms, with some of the pieces having been made by Frances's father, an Episcopal minister.

Her father's ministerial duties kept the family away from Edenton while Frances was growing up, except for three special times of the year—a few days after Christmas, in spring during the shad and herring season, and a few weeks in the summer.

At Christmas, Frances's mother would serve roast goose at one end of the table and baked ham at the other. In between were rice, corn, peas, snap beans, whole cranberry sauce, celery, olives, and beaten biscuits, Frances says. For dessert, she served a favorite English Yuletide dish—plum pudding.

In the spring, her mother returned to Edenton during the herring and shad season. Frances recalls, "Some of the happiest times of my mother's childhood had been spent down at the fishery." During those days of ample herring and shad, the family ate fish three times a day. Some of that liking for herring

35

rubbed off on Frances, who admits to having "an inordinate fondness for herring roe."

During the family's summer visits, they ate the fresh vegetables and fruits that were available in abundance in that season.

Frances acquired more than a taste for herring from her family. She stills refers to a handwritten family cookbook compiled by her mother during the 1920s. From it, she stirs up plum pudding, homemade tomato catsup, and rock muddle. And recently, a family member discovered another family cookbook that dates back to the 1860s. It was donated to the Edenton Historical Society for display and historical use. A few of the recipes found in its pages appear among Frances's collection.

BAKED SHAD

1 4- to 5-pound female shad, dressed, with roe
   (do not remove roe from fish)
1 teaspoon salt
¼ teaspoon black pepper
½ cup catsup

Place shad on a greased baking sheet. Salt and pepper and top with catsup. Bake in a 350-degree oven 15 minutes per inch of thickness of fish or until a fork can be easily inserted in the thickest part of fish. Serves 4.

ROCK MUDDLE

3 to 4 slices bacon
2 medium onions, diced
3 to 4 medium Irish potatoes, diced
water
1 3-pound rockfish (striped bass), dressed, skinned, and cut into chunks

ROE

Some say the best caviar is the roe of the sturgeon. Coastal Carolinians are sure to disagree. When prepared correctly, the fish eggs of mullet, menhaden, shad, and herring are just as tasty, they say.

The roe usually consist of two elongated sacklike ovaries, covered with a connective membrane. The color varies according to species, ranging from yellow to orange to black.

The eggs of each species have a distinctive taste and texture. Descriptions of the variations in flavor will not suffice; you must try the roe for yourself. And even roe-lovers warn that it is a taste you have to acquire.

Most roes are good fried, baked, dried, or scrambled with eggs. If roe are plentiful, cooks often serve them alone as the main dish.

1 teaspoon salt
½ teaspoon black pepper
1 tablespoon Worcestershire sauce

In a saucepan, render grease from bacon. Remove meat and set aside. Add onions and sauté until clear. Add potatoes and cover with water. Bring to a boil, reduce heat, and simmer until potatoes are tender. Add fish, salt, pepper, and Worcestershire sauce. Do not stir. Simmer 15 minutes longer. Crumble bacon and sprinkle over muddle. Serves 4.

FRIED HERRING ROE

12 herring roe
½ cup cornmeal
½ teaspoon salt

½ teaspoon black pepper
vegetable oil

Dip roe in cornmeal. Salt and pepper. Lightly grease a large skillet with vegetable oil. Place roe in skillet and panfry over medium heat, 10 minutes per side. Serves 4.

BAKED SHAD ROE

4 shad roe
3 slices bacon, chopped
1 lemon

Place roe on an ungreased baking sheet. Top with chopped bacon. Bake for 30 minutes in a 350-degree oven. Serve with lemon slices or wedges. Serves 4.

FISH PIE

This recipe comes from Mary M. C. Littlejohn, another of Frances's ancestors, who was born in Edenton in 1841. Mary used the bones left from her cooked fish to flavor the stock.

fish bones
2½ cups water
4 tablespoons butter
6 tablespoons flour
1 egg
1 heaping teaspoon anchovy paste
1 teaspoon lemon juice
½ teaspoon salt
¼ teaspoon black pepper
1 pound cooked, flaked fish, any species
3 cups cooked mashed potatoes

In a saucepan, place fish bones and water. Boil 20 minutes. Remove from heat and cool. Strain bones from stock. In another saucepan, melt butter over medium heat. Add flour and mix. Add ½ cup of cooled stock and stir vigorously until well mixed. Remove from heat and add egg, anchovy paste, lemon juice, salt, and pepper. Mix. Add fish and combine. In a deep-dish pie pan, spread 1½ cups of mashed potatoes. Then spread fish mixture. Top with remaining mashed potatoes. Spread evenly. Bake in a 350-degree oven for 20 minutes. Serves 4 to 6.

ROASTED GOOSE

1½ teaspoons salt
½ teaspoon black pepper
1 10- to 14-pound goose, cleaned
2 stalks celery, coarsely chopped
1 apple, quartered
1 onion, quartered

Salt and pepper inside and outside of goose. Place celery, apple, and onion in the cavity of the goose. Truss legs. Turn back wings and secure with kitchen string. Prick skin. Place goose in a roasting pan and place in a 450-degree oven. Immediately reduce the heat to 350 degrees. Bake 20 minutes per pound of meat.

HOMEMADE CATSUP

1 peck tomatoes, quartered
6 large onions, quartered
3 tablespoons black pepper
2 tablespoons dry mustard
2 cups vinegar
3 tablespoons salt
1 tablespoon celery salt
½ cup sugar (optional)
1 to 2 hot pepper pods
sterilized pint jars

This was Frances's grandmother's recipe. She used measurements such as a "dessert spoonful," which Frances has converted into modern measurements. Unlike her grandmother, Frances does not add sugar to her catsup.

MARKET FORMS

Fresh fish is available in a variety of forms in the market. Most recipes will indicate whether a particular form is necessary and whether you can substitute other forms.

- Whole or round fish are sold just as they come from the water. They must be scaled and eviscerated before cooking. If the head is left on, the fish must be degilled. The edible yield is about 45 percent.
- Drawn fish have been eviscerated. They must be scaled and, if the head is left on, degilled. The edible portion is about 48 percent.

- Dressed fish are ready to cook, usually with the head, tail, and fins removed. The edible portion is about 67 percent.
- Steaks are ready-to-cook cross-sectional slices of large fish. The edible yield is about 86 percent.
- Fillets are the sides of the fish cut away from the backbone and are ready to cook. They are usually boneless, with no waste.
- Butterfly fillets are the two single fillets held together by the uncut belly skin. They contain the few bones from the rib cage.

The amount of seafood a cook allows per

In a 6- to 8-quart pot, combine tomatoes and onions. Simmer until tender. Sieve to make 1 gallon tomato juice. Return juice to pot and add black pepper, dry mustard, vinegar, salt, celery salt, sugar, and pepper pods. Stirring frequently, boil until catsup becomes very thick, about one-half the original quantity. Remove from heat, and discard pepper pods. Pour catsup into sterilized pint jars, leaving a ½-inch air space at the top. Seal and process 10 minutes in a boiling-water bath.

person depends upon the market form. Since the edible yield of whole or round fish is only about 45 percent, most recipes require ¾ pound per serving, based on about 3 ounces per serving. Recipes calling for dressed fish usually allow ½ pound per serving. Fillets and steaks, which have little waste, require ⅓ pound for a serving.

For oysters and clams in the shell, the general rule is 6 per person. If the mollusks are shucked, ⅙ pint will suffice. A quarter of a pound of scallops will feed one person.

Cooks should allow ¼ pound cooked crab meat per person and 1 to 2 pounds of live crabs. Most recipes call for half a pound of headed shrimp or ¼ pound of cooked and peeled shrimp.

The amounts may vary, depending on the recipe and the other ingredients in it. Stews and chowders, for instance, that contain vegetables or dumplings, may call for less seafood.

Note: This information was provided by Joyce Taylor, UNC Sea Grant's seafood specialist at the North Carolina State University Seafood Laboratory in Morehead City.

TOMATO SAUCE

2 dozen large, ripe tomatoes
1 large green pepper, diced
2 large or 3 small onions, diced
3 cloves garlic, minced
½ cup fresh parsley, minced
2 tablespoons fresh basil, minced
2 tablespoons fresh oregano, minced
2 bay leaves, crushed

This is best, Frances says, when made from fresh ingredients from your garden. She says you can vary the combination of herbs according to taste.

1 red pepper pod or 1 teaspoon black pepper
1 tablespoon salt
sterilized pint jars or freezer containers

Scald, skin, and quarter tomatoes. Combine tomatoes, green pepper, onions, garlic, parsley, basil,
oregano, bay leaves, pepper pod or black pepper,
and salt in a 6-quart steel pot. Bring to boil, reduce
heat, and simmer 15 minutes, longer if you prefer a
thick sauce.

If using pepper pods, remove prior to preserving.
Freeze in freezer containers or put into hot, sterilized
jars. Process jars for 35 minutes at 10 pounds of
pressure in pressure cooker. Use as a soup base.

CORN DODGERS

1 cup cornmeal
1 teaspoon salt
¾ cup boiling water

In a mixing bowl, combine cornmeal and salt. Stir in
boiling water. Cover and set aside for 10 minutes.
Shape into thumb-size nuggets and place on a
greased baking pan. Bake at 350 degrees for 45 minutes. Makes 18 to 24.

EGG BREAD

1 cup water-ground cornmeal
1 teaspoon baking powder
3 eggs
2 cups milk
2 tablespoons butter

In a mixing bowl, sift meal with baking powder. In
another bowl, beat together eggs and milk. Stir into

dry ingredients. Melt butter in a 1-quart baking dish. Then rub butter around inside of baking dish, being sure to coat the sides and bottom evenly. Pour in batter and stir. Bake in a 350-degree oven for 35 minutes or until a knife inserted in the center comes out clean. Serve hot with butter.

BEATEN BISCUITS

2 cups flour
½ teaspoon salt
2 tablespoons shortening or lard
½ to 1 cup ice water (use as little as possible)

In a mixing bowl, combine flour and salt. Cut in shortening or lard until mixture reaches consistency of cornmeal. Add just enough water to form the dough into a loose ball. Turn dough out onto a floured board. Knead and beat dough until satiny. Using a floured rolling pin, roll the dough to ¼-inch thickness. Cut into small biscuits, using a small snuff can or 2-inch diameter biscuit cutter. Place on a greased baking sheet, and bake at 400 degrees for 20 minutes. Lower heat to 275 degrees and bake 1 hour.

Beaten biscuits have a texture almost like thick crackers, Frances says. She uses an old biscuit break to make them, running the crumbly dough through the break until it becomes satiny. But those who do not own one of these old-time apparatuses can achieve the same results by kneading the dough and beating it with a mallet.

ARTICHOKE PICKLES

1 peck Jerusalem artichokes
3 pounds onions, sliced
sterilized quart jars
6 to 8 red pepper pods (optional)
3 quarts vinegar
5 pounds sugar
2 tablespoons turmeric
2 tablespoons dry mustard

Frances says drying the washed artichokes with a towel is the secret to crisp pickles. Also, Frances does not process her pickles in a boiling-water bath because she does not want to reduce their crispness. But home economists advise processing the pickles. They say that if you begin counting your pro-

cessing time as soon as you place the jars in the bath, crispness will not be reduced.

Put artichokes and onions in alternating layers in jars. For hot pickles, add 1 hot pepper pod per jar. Boil together vinegar, sugar, and remaining spices for 5 minutes and pour over artichokes and onions, leaving a 1-inch air space. Seal and process 10 minutes in a boiling-water bath. Makes 6 to 8 quarts.

LEMON CHESS PIE

Frances cautions that this chess pie should be watched closely while it bakes to prevent over-cooking. Make sure the delicate crust that forms on top is tan, not brown, she says. Bake just until the center is barely firm.

2 cups sugar
⅛ teaspoon salt
1 tablespoon cornmeal
1 tablespoon flour
¼ cup melted butter
grated rind and juice of 2 lemons
½ cup milk
4 eggs
1 9-inch unbaked pie shell

In a mixing bowl, mix sugar, salt, cornmeal, and flour. In a small saucepan, melt butter. Cool slightly. Add lemon juice and rind, cooled butter, and milk to dry ingredients. Mix. Add eggs one at a time and incorporate thoroughly. Pour into an unbaked pie shell. Bake in a 350-degree oven for 40 minutes.

APPLE CRISP

2 quarts sliced apples, unpeeled
1 teaspoon cinnamon
½ teaspoon ground nutmeg
1 stick butter
½ cup whole wheat flour
1 cup oatmeal
1½ cups brown sugar

Place apples in a baking dish and sprinkle with cinnamon and nutmeg. In a skillet, melt butter. To butter, add flour, oatmeal, and brown sugar. Pat oatmeal and flour mixture over apples. Bake in a 350-degree oven for 1 hour.

BLIGHT HOUSE PLUM PUDDING

1½ pounds currants
1½ pounds raisins
1 pound dried citron
1 pound bread or cracker crumbs
10 eggs, separated
1 pound brown sugar
1 pound suet or creamed butter, soft
¾ cup brandy
¾ cup sherry
1 teaspoon ground nutmeg
2 teaspoons cinnamon
2 teaspoons ground allspice
1½ teaspoons ground cloves
1½ teaspoons mace
juice of 1 lemon
1 teaspoon grated lemon rind
kitchen string

This Yuletide dessert keeps well, according to Frances. In fact, she says, the flavor is better if the pudding is made two weeks prior to serving.

In a large mixing bowl, mix fruit. Add bread crumbs. The fruit and crumbs may be mixed the day before cooking.

In a second large mixing bowl, beat egg yolks. To the yolks, add sugar and suet or butter. Add brandy, sherry, spices, lemon juice, and grated rind. Mix. In another large mixing bowl, beat egg whites until stiff. Fold egg whites into yolk mixture, and then add fruit and crumbs.

Grease a pudding mold. Pack the pudding into the mold, leaving room for expansion. Cover with wax paper and secure with kitchen string. Place mold on a trivet in a pot of boiling water. Cover and steam for 5 hours; additional water may be needed. Cool and serve with the following sauce.

Sauce

1 egg, separated
½ cup powdered sugar, sifted
¼ cup cream, whipped
1 teaspoon vanilla or 1 tablespoon dark rum
   or sherry

In a small mixing bowl, beat egg white until stiff. Stir in sifted powdered sugar. Add egg yolk and beat until light. Fold in whipped cream. Flavor with vanilla, rum, or sherry.

JEANIE WILLIAMS
Manteo

J eanie Williams cooks "by guessing by gosh."
That's the phrase her husband used when he
found her adding a pinch of this and a handful of that to his evening meals. "He asked me why I
didn't use recipes," she says. "I told him I couldn't
read and cook at the same time. 'Well then,' he says,
'if you guess and it turns out good, it's a miracle by
gosh.' "

If that's the case, Jeanie has turned out more than
her fair share of miracles. Reared on the Outer Banks
at Avon, Jeanie still prepares some of the same
dishes she grew up eating—roasted swan, clam
chowder, and mashed rutabagas.

When she cooks vegetables, Jeanie always adds a
tablespoon of sugar. "People around here make fun
of me for using so much sugar," she says. "But I like
my vegetables sweet."

Her family mixed fishing, farming, and hunting to
keep food on the table. Though her father was a fisherman, he kept a vegetable garden, cows for milk,
and hogs for meat.

"Keeping" hogs on the Banks was different from
keeping hogs inland. Each hog was branded on the
ear and then set free to roam for its meals. "They ate
everything in sight," Jeanie says.

ROASTED SWAN

1 swan, 8 to 12 pounds, plucked and dressed
3 tablespoons vegetable oil or shortening
1 tablespoon salt
1 teaspoon black pepper

Rub skin of swan with oil or shortening. Salt and
pepper. Place swan in 1 inch of water in a covered

*Jeanie says the cooking
time will depend on the
size and age of the bird.
A larger swan or an
older swan will require
more cooking time. You
can tell the age of the
bird by the number of
pin feathers it has, she
says. Younger birds have
more pin feathers.*

47

roasting pan. Roast in a 325-degree oven 3 to 3½ hours, until the juices run clear when the bird is pierced at the upper thigh or a meat thermometer registers 185 degrees. Serves 8 to 10.

CLAM CHOWDER WITH RICE

Freezing clams makes them easier to open and allows the cook to save the clam meat and juices. And, Jeanie says, "There's no need for much salt. The clam's own natural juices have plenty of salt." In fact, Jeanie adds rice to reduce some of the saltiness.

24 medium to large clams, frozen
1 slice salt pork
4 cups water
4 medium Irish potatoes, diced
2 medium onions, chopped
½ teaspoon black pepper
2 tablespoons uncooked rice

While the clams are frozen, open the shells and remove the contents. Chop, saving the juices.

In a 2-quart saucepan, render the fat from the salt pork. Remove pork. Add clams, clam juice, water, potatoes, onions, pepper, and rice. Bring to a boil, cover, and reduce heat. Simmer for 1½ hours. Serves 4.

BLUEFISH CAKES

Jeanie often begins with frozen bluefish. After removing the fish from the freezer, she sprinkles it with one cup of salt and lets it stand overnight in the refrigerator. She rinses the fish thoroughly the next day before making her cakes.

1 3- to 4-pound bluefish, dressed
water
2 Irish potatoes, peeled and diced
1 onion, diced
½ teaspoon salt
½ teaspoon black pepper
½ cup plain flour
2 tablespoons vegetable oil

In a large saucepan, cover bluefish with water and bring to a boil. Cover and simmer until the fish flakes. Drain. Remove the fish from the skin and bones, and flake. Meanwhile, boil potatoes until

CLAM SIZES

Clams come in three sizes: chowder, cherrystone, and littleneck. The chowder clam is the largest and least expensive. It is chopped for chowder or fritters. The cherrystone, a medium-sized hard clam which is moderately priced, is served raw or steamed. The littleneck, the small-est and most expensive hard clam, is served raw on the half shell or steamed.

tender. Mix together flaked bluefish, potatoes, and raw onion. Season with salt and pepper. Shape into patties. Roll in flour. Panfry in oil over medium high heat. Makes 12 to 14 cakes.

MASHED RUTABAGAS

1 to 2 thin slices salt pork
1½ pounds rutabagas, peeled and sliced
1 tablespoon sugar
water

Render the fat from the salt pork in a 2-quart pot. Remove pork. Add rutabagas and sugar. Cover with water. Bring to a boil, reduce heat, and simmer until tender. Drain. Using a potato masher or fork, mash rutabagas. Serves 4.

MASHED TURNIPS

1½ pounds turnips, peeled and sliced
water
1 tablespoon sugar
2 tablespoons butter

Place sliced turnips in a 2-quart pot. Cover with water. Add sugar. Bring to a boil, then reduce heat and simmer until tender. Drain. To hot turnips, add butter. Mash turnips with potato masher or fork. Serves 4.

STEWED TOMATOES

Jeanie uses tomatoes she has canned herself, but she says store-bought tomatoes can be used. But don't expect the store-bought variety to be as flavorful, she warns. Stewed tomatoes are delicious served with fried herring roe (recipe, page 37).

1 quart canned tomatoes and juice
1 tablespoon sugar
2 cold biscuits, crumbled
1 tablespoon butter

Pour tomatoes and juice into a 2-quart saucepan. Add sugar, crumbled biscuits, and butter. Bring to a rolling boil. Remove from heat and serve warm. Serves 4.

STRING BEANS WITH POTATOES AND CORNMEAL DUMPLINGS

Jeanie recommends Kentucky Wonder beans. Her father and husband raised that variety, and she believes they have more flavor.

1 pound fresh string beans
water
1 ham bone
6 to 8 new potatoes, halved
cornmeal dumplings (recipes, pp. 104, 116, and 138)

Snap beans. Place in a medium saucepan and cover with water. Add a ham bone that has some meat on it to flavor the beans. Cover and simmer for 2 to 3 hours. Additional water may be needed during cooking. One hour before serving, add potatoes. Twenty minutes before serving, remove bone and add cornmeal dumplings. Serves 4.

YEAST ROLLS

1 tablespoon yeast
1 cup warm water
1 teaspoon sugar
4½ cups plain flour
½ cup boiling water
2 tablespoons instant potatoes
3 tablespoons butter or margarine
½ cup powdered milk
½ cup sugar
1 teaspoon salt
1 egg, beaten
4 tablespoons softened butter

When making these yeast rolls, Jeanie punches down the rising dough every time she passes through the kitchen. She believes this makes for a finer-textured bread. Jeanie begins the dough in the morning and shapes it into rolls about two hours before dinner. Her hands serve as her utensils. "I don't have a thing to wash but my hands," she says.

In a mixing bowl, dissolve yeast in warm water. Combine 1 teaspoon sugar and ½ cup flour and add to yeast mixture. Allow to sit for 15 minutes. To ½ cup of boiling water, add instant potatoes and 3 tablespoons of butter. Stir. In another mixing bowl, combine powdered milk, 4 cups of flour, ½ cup sugar, and salt; form a well. Add egg, potato mixture, and yeast mixture to the well. Combine. You may need to add extra warm water if the dough does not hold together or appears dry.

Turn the dough onto a board and knead for 10 minutes or until it no longer sticks to your hands. Extra flour may be needed. Place dough in a warm spot to let it rise. Punch the dough down from time to time.

Two hours prior to your meal, grease two cookie sheets with shortening. Punch the dough down and knead briefly. Pinch off small handfuls of dough and shape into small ovals. Roll each in softened butter and place on cookie sheet about 3 inches apart. Leave the rolls in a warm spot and allow them to double in size (about 1½ hours). Place in a 450-degree oven; bake until golden brown, about 15 minutes. Makes 24 to 30 rolls.

When Jeanie's grand-
children are scheduled
for a visit, she knows to
put a pan full of sticky
rolls on the menu for
breakfast. The dough is
the same as her yeast
rolls.

STICKY BUNS

dough (follow recipe for yeast rolls, above)
1 stick butter, softened
1½ cups brown sugar
2 teaspoons cinnamon
¾ cup honey or corn syrup
1 cup chopped pecans

Instead of forming rolls with the dough, roll it out
into a rectangle (12 inches × 18 inches) about
¼ inch to ½ inch thick. Spread half of a stick of
softened butter onto the dough. Sprinkle with ¾ cup
of brown sugar and cinnamon. Dribble on honey or
corn syrup. Roll up the dough lengthwise like a jelly
roll. Cut into 1-inch slices. Melt the other half-stick
of butter and pour into the bottom of a large baking
pan. Over butter, sprinkle remaining brown sugar
and pecans. Place rolls in the pan.

Place rolls in a warm spot and allow to double in
size. Place in a 400-degree oven and bake until
golden brown. Lift rolls out of pan with a spatula and
flip over. The gooey bottom surface will be the top
of the roll. Makes 24 to 30 rolls.

CHOCOLATE POUND CAKE

3 cups plain flour
½ cup cocoa
½ teaspoon baking powder
½ teaspoon salt
2 sticks butter
½ cup shortening
3 cups sugar
5 eggs
1¼ cups milk
1 teaspoon vanilla

In a bowl, sift together flour, cocoa, baking powder, and salt. In a large mixing bowl, cream butter, shortening, and sugar until fluffy. Add eggs one at a time, beating well after each one. Add sifted ingredients alternately with milk. Add vanilla. Pour batter into a greased and floured tube pan. Bake at 325 degrees for 1½ hours.

NORA SCARBOROUGH
Wanchese

Once a month in the summertime, Nora Scarborough, her family, and thirty-five or forty friends leave the relaxed atmosphere of Wanchese for a day of more of the same. They pile into boats and head for Portsmouth Island, just southeast of Ocracoke Island. Part of the National Park Service's Cape Lookout National Seashore, the community of Portsmouth is deserted now. All that remains are buildings that hark back to the days when the village was an important shipping point.

But the bounty of the waters around Portsmouth remains. Even today, recreational fishermen from all along the East Coast come to the deserted island to cast lines into the Atlantic and reel in some of the biggest, most delicious fish around. Nora and her friends don't even bother to take many groceries on their outings because they know there will be plenty of food when they get there. A few rods and reels yield enough channel bass for frying, and a couple of clam rakes turn over enough clams for stewing a chowder.

A day at Portsmouth reminds Nora of her growing-up years in Hatteras. She would walk the shore along the sound, searching for soft-shell crabs hiding in the grassy lumps. "You had to be quick, though. The birds would find them quick as a flash," says Nora.

When she moved to Wanchese forty-five years ago, it took some time for Nora to get used to the seafood pulled from Albemarle Sound. "There's too much fresh water in the sounds here," she explains. Hatteras seafood, by contrast, is saltier and tastier, she claims.

She has had time to adjust, though. Now, she says, "I love seafood better than any other."

CRAB SOUP

2 slices salt pork
4 medium Irish potatoes, diced
½ cup rice, uncooked
1 medium onion, diced
12 whole hard crabs, steamed and cleaned
  (with roe, if desired)
water

In a 6- to 10-quart pot, render fat from salt pork. Remove pork. Add remaining ingredients and cover with water. Simmer over medium heat for 1 hour. Serves 4.

In the springtime, Nora uses female crabs and their eggs to make "she-crab" soup. The eggs are those inside the female, not the egg sac outside under the apron. You should serve crab soup with plenty of napkins alongside; you will be cracking the crabs at the table.

CRAB CAKES

1 pound cooked crab claw meat
2 eggs, beaten
1 teaspoon salt
½ teaspoon black pepper
1 tablespoon mayonnaise
1 teaspoon Worcestershire sauce
½ cup cracker meal
¾ cup vegetable oil

In a bowl, combine first seven ingredients. Using hands, form mixture into cakes. In a skillet, panfry in hot oil until golden brown on both sides. Serves 6.

Some people add onion and green pepper to their crab cakes. But Nora says this detracts from the natural flavor of the crab meat. "I want the real taste," she says. Nora uses this same recipe to make hors d'oeuvres for parties. She shapes the mixture into small balls and deep-fries them.

When fresh tuna is available, Nora substitutes it in this crab cake recipe.

FRESH TUNA FISH SALAD

1 pound cooked tuna
2 hard-boiled eggs, diced
1 small onion, diced
1 tablespoon sweet pickle relish
3 to 4 tablespoons mayonnaise

In a mixing bowl, combine ingredients. Serve on a bed of lettuce or as a sandwich. Serves 6 to 8.

RAW OYSTERS

Nora recommends eating oysters raw. And no crackers for her. If they are good oysters, they are best by themselves. She adds, "I have to open my own oysters. I don't like them if somebody else opens them for me. They don't taste as good." Her method for shucking an oyster: Insert an oyster knife into the mouth, at the front part of the oyster. With a twisting motion, run the blade around the oyster until it cuts the muscle, which is located near the hinge. Nora recommends harvesting oysters on an incoming tide. They are saltier then, she says.

STEWED SHRIMP

2 pounds shrimp, headed and peeled
4 medium Irish potatoes, diced
1 medium onion, diced
water
2 tablespoons cornstarch or cornmeal dumplings
 (recipes, pp. 104, 116, and 138)

In a large saucepan, combine shrimp, potatoes, and onions. Cover with water and simmer over medium heat for 30 minutes. Thicken with cornstarch or add cornmeal dumplings and cook an additional 20 minutes. Serves 4 to 6.

OYSTER DRESSING FOR TURKEY

1 box saltine crackers, crushed
2 sticks butter, melted
1 stalk celery, diced
1 medium onion, chopped
1 tablespoon sage
1 teaspoon black pepper
1 pint whole oysters and their juices
giblets, optional (cooked and chopped)

If there is any dressing left over after stuffing the turkey, Nora cooks it in a pan and serves it separately.

In a mixing bowl, combine ingredients. Stuff in turkey's cavity and bake turkey as directed.

LUCILLE OSBORNE
Engelhard

Every now and then, as she shuffles through her old recipes, Lucille Osborne comes across a scrap of paper with a menu scribbled on it. Turkey, dressing, snap beans, baked tomatoes, and raw apple cake—for fifty hungry hunters. The scraps of paper are memories of the twelve years Lucille and her husband managed the Mattamuskeet Lodge on Lake Mattamuskeet in Hyde County. The lodge accommodated up to fifty-five hunters, fishermen, bird watchers, or schoolchildren.

In addition to maintaining the lodge, Lucille spent most of her time keeping her guests pleased at dinnertime. That meant planning menus, deciding on recipes, ordering groceries, and cooking and serving the meals. Each day tested her organizational skills, says Lucille. Breakfast for the hunters—served promptly at five o'clock in the morning—consisted of the usual eggs, bacon, sausage, grits, and toast or biscuits. And on their way out to the blinds, the hunters picked up the bag lunches they had ordered the night before. For the extra-cold days, Lucille prepared as many as fifty thermoses filled with hot chicken soup, vegetable soup, and coffee or tea.

In the evenings, the fifty-some guests gathered around tables that had been built by workers in the Civilian Conservation Corps camps in the 1930s. Waitresses served them food with a southern coastal flair. In all her years there, Lucille says only one guest from the North objected to her way of cooking and serving food.

To keep her pantry stocked, Lucille ordered groceries once a week from the meat man, the vegetable man, and the egg man when they delivered the weekly supplies.

Now that the lodge is closed, Lucille and her husband live in a house in Engelhard just across the street from where she grew up. She remembers when her father used to feed the shrimp he caught in his nets to the hogs. Her father fished, farmed, and served as the local blacksmith, shoeing horses and sharpening plow points. Lucille and her brother spent most of their days picking cotton for a little extra money or fishing in Middle Creek which wound behind the house and fed into Pamlico Sound. When the sound would freeze over in the winter, they would break the ice and scoop up the fish that surfaced for air.

BAKED COUNTRY HAM

Lucille likes to serve baked country ham with potato salad and string beans.

1 10- to 12-pound country ham
water

Wash the ham and place it in a large roasting pan. Add 1 inch of water in the bottom. Cover and bake in a 325-degree oven for 4 hours. Additional water may be needed. Slice and serve.

FRIED PORK CHOPS

1 teaspoon salt
½ teaspoon black pepper
1 cup plain flour
4 pork chops
¼ cup vegetable oil

Salt and pepper flour. Dredge pork chops in seasoned flour. Panfry in hot oil over medium heat. Cook ½-inch thick chops 5 minutes each side and 1-inch chops 10 minutes each side. Serves 4.

CHICKEN SOUP WITH VEGETABLES

1 whole chicken, cleaned and cut up
water
1 stalk celery, diced
2 carrots, diced
1 medium onion, diced
2 medium Irish potatoes, diced
½ cup rice, uncooked
½ cup macaroni noodles, uncooked
1 teaspoon salt
½ teaspoon black pepper

In a medium saucepan, cover chicken with water and bring to a boil. Reduce heat and simmer for 1 hour until chicken is tender. Remove chicken from stock, cool, and cut into bite-sized pieces. Return chicken to the stock and add remaining ingredients. Simmer 30 minutes. Serves 6.

MASHED POTATOES

6 medium Irish potatoes, peeled and quartered
water
1 stick butter or margarine
½ to ¾ cup milk
2 teaspoons salt

In a large saucepan, cover potatoes with water and boil until tender. Drain excess water. Add butter, milk, and salt and beat with an electric mixer until potatoes are smooth. Serves 4.

BAKED TOMATOES

6 slices of bread, toasted
28 to 32 ounces canned whole tomatoes, chopped

2 tablespoons butter or margarine
2 tablespoons sugar

Crumble toast into an 8 × 10-inch baking dish. Spread evenly across the bottom of the dish. Spread tomatoes over toast. Top with pats of butter and sprinkle with sugar. Bake at 350 degrees for 30 minutes. Serves 4.

LACY CORN BREAD

1 cup white cornmeal
1¾ cups water
1 small onion, chopped fine
1 teaspoon salt
¼ teaspoon black pepper
½ cup vegetable oil

In a large mixing bowl, combine cornmeal, water, onion, and seasonings. Mix well. Drop batter by the tablespoonful into hot oil in a large skillet. Allow 2 tablespoons for each corn cake. Brown well on both sides. Drain on paper towels. Makes 2 dozen cakes.

RAW APPLE CAKE

2 cups sugar
1¼ cups vegetable oil
2 cups plain flour
3 eggs
1 teaspoon salt
1 teaspoon baking soda
1 teaspoon vanilla
1 teaspoon cinnamon
3 cups raw apples, peeled and diced
1 cup pecans, chopped

CORNMEAL

When the Indians taught the first settlers how to grow corn, they provided the settlers with more than a fresh vegetable. They provided a meal—cornmeal, that is. The settlers quickly learned how to make cornmeal into corn bread, pone bread, spoonbread, and dumplings, and they coated fish, shellfish, and some vegetables with it prior to frying.

Cornmeal has always been a major ingredient in southern fare. Corn was easier to cultivate and more productive than wheat, which did not grow well in the soggy South. Corn was also easier to grind with the crude machinery that was usually available during the early days of settlement. And it was easier and faster to make cornmeal into corn bread than it was to make flour into bread. Commercial baking powder was unavailable until the mid-1880s, and so cooks had to use yeast to "raise" wheat flour.

As late as the mid-1930s, the average southern family consumed five hundred pounds of cornmeal a year as compared to about one hundred pounds in the rest of the country.

Cornmeal is still popular today. Some cooks swear by white cornmeal; others, yellow. For some cornmeal connoisseurs, only fine-ground meal will do, while others prefer coarse-ground. Many cooks stand as faithfully and as fervently by certain brands of cornmeal as they stand by the American flag. To stress that point, many of the cooks we interviewed went to their pantries to pull out bags of cornmeal for our inspection.

In a large mixing bowl, cream sugar and oil by hand. Add remaining ingredients and mix well. Pour batter into a greased tube pan. Bake 1 hour and 15 minutes at 300 degrees.

PINEAPPLE UPSIDE-DOWN CAKE

1 stick butter or margarine
1 cup brown sugar
1 15-ounce can sliced pineapple (about 5 rings) and
   juices, separated (reserve juice for batter recipe)
cake batter (see below)

In an iron skillet, melt butter and brown sugar. Arrange pineapple in the skillet. Pour batter over pineapple. Bake for 30 minutes at 325 degrees or until a toothpick comes out clean. Cool and turn out onto a large platter, fruit side up.

Batter
½ cup butter, room temperature
1 cup sugar
2 eggs
juice from pineapple
1½ cups self-rising flour
½ cup water

In a mixing bowl, cream butter and sugar. Add eggs, one at a time, then juice from pineapple. Add flour and water alternately.

SARAH LATHAM
Belhaven

Every Sunday, eighty-five-year-old Sarah Latham serves the noon meal to fifteen to twenty members of her family. "That's one way to keep up with them," she says. When her grandchildren praise her cooking, she disclaims her abilities in the kitchen: "They only think I'm a good cook because they love to eat so much."

Sarah lives in Belhaven now, but she grew up a few miles away in Pantego—"the greatest little town you ever heard of. Everybody knows everybody's business and tends to it. Belhaven is too big for that," she says. There was a time, when she sold insurance for nearly twenty-five years, that she knew everybody in the county, she says.

Sarah's father was sixty years old when he married her twenty-two-year-old mother. "It's good for old and young blood to mix," she says. Her father, who died when she was nine, was a man of many occupations —farmer, disciple minister, blacksmith, land surveyor, and blockade runner.

When Sarah was young, her family moved from the country to Pantego so the children could go to the best school in the county. The teacher taught out of her home, and her front yard served as playground and cafeteria. At lunchtime, the students took their bags outside and sat on the ground to eat. Pork sandwiches were standard fare for most of the children, but Sarah and her brothers and sisters always had collard biscuits—a spoonful of collards wrapped inside a big biscuit and sprinkled with pepper vinegar. For variety, they would swap their collard biscuits for a pork sandwich.

Sarah's favorite breakfast meal consisted of chunks of sharp cheese dropped into a large mug of hot coffee. She dipped the melted cheese and coffee with a spoon and combined it with toast and jam.

"You ought to try it," she says, whistling to indicate its good flavor. For the best flavor, Sarah uses a half cup of cheese to a cup of coffee.

When Sarah was seventeen, she married and moved to her husband's family's farm near Belhaven. Her father-in-law was a farmer and an experimenter; he developed Latham double-ear seed corn, a variety that resulted in fewer but larger ears of corn per stalk.

Sarah's mother-in-law was a businesswoman, too. She raised money for herself and the church by raising turkeys. "Whenever it rained, we would rush to get the turkeys inside because they would stand with their necks stretched up and their mouths wide open until they drowned," says Sarah.

Sarah gives all the credit for her cooking ability to her mother. "She was the beatingest cook you've ever seen," she says. Now, when she needs a recipe, she consults a cookbook she has scribbled in since 1920.

FRIED BUTTERFISH

1 teaspoon salt
½ teaspoon black pepper
3 pounds dressed butterfish
3 eggs, beaten
1 cup cornmeal
1 cup shortening

Salt and pepper butterfish. Dip fish in egg, then in cornmeal, coating evenly with the meal. Panfry in hot shortening in a large skillet over medium heat, browning both sides. Serves 6.

Sarah says butterfish taste better than any other fish she has ever had. She likes them best panfried.

Sarah says one 15-pound ham will feed as many as thirty people if you have plenty of side dishes.

BAKED SUGAR-CURED HAM

1 15-pound sugar-cured ham
water

Place ham, fat-side down, in a large roasting pan. Add 1 inch of water in the bottom. Cover with a tent of aluminum foil. Bake at 300 degrees, 20 minutes to the pound, or about 5 hours. After the first three hours, turn ham and continue baking. To serve, trim away excess fat. Slice thin.

Sarah fries her chicken at eight o'clock in the morning on the day that she plans to serve it. Then she lines a baking pan with a paper bag and paper towels over that. She places the chicken on the paper towels to absorb any excess grease. When it is time to eat, she puts the chicken back into the oven to warm while she cooks her biscuits.

FRIED CHICKEN

2 cups plain flour
1 whole chicken, cleaned and cut up
½ cup bacon grease
½ cup shortening
salt
black pepper

Place flour in a plastic or paper bag. Drop chicken pieces into the bag one at a time and shake, coating each piece evenly with flour. Heat bacon grease and shortening in a large skillet over medium heat. Place chicken in skillet and sprinkle each piece with salt and pepper. Fry 30 minutes on each side. Remove from pan and place on paper towels to absorb grease. Serves 4.

Sarah always freezes her leftover chicken stock so she will have it on hand for dishes like her baked chicken dressing. The secret to this recipe, she says, is the celery seed. She

BAKED CHICKEN DRESSING

4 cups corn bread, crumbled
2 cups toasted bread crumbs
1 cup chicken stock
1 cup water

1 to 2 tablespoons celery seed
1 tablespoon Worcestershire sauce
1 tablespoon Tabasco
2 tablespoons A-1 sauce

never uses fresh celery because it softens too much.

Place crumbled corn bread and toast in a large mixing bowl. Add chicken stock, water, and remaining ingredients. Mix well. Spoon mixture into a 9 × 12-inch ungreased baking pan. Bake at 350 degrees until dressing browns. Serves 8.

HAM ROLLS

2 yeast cakes
½ cup sugar
1 tablespoon salt
⅔ cup shortening
2 cups water, boiled and cooled to lukewarm
2 eggs
8 cups plain flour
slices of ham

When she has leftover ham, Sarah makes ham rolls. "And there's only two kinds of flour you can use—hard wheat flours like Pillsbury or Gold Medal," she says.

In a large mixing bowl, combine yeast, sugar, salt, and shortening. Add water and blend. Stir in eggs and beat lightly with a mixer. Still using the mixer, begin to add flour. When the dough becomes too stiff for the mixer, slowly add the remaining flour, working with hands. Knead dough well. Place in a greased bowl in a warm place and let rise to three times its size. Knead dough again and shape into rolls. Place on a greased baking pan and let rolls rise again. Bake at 400 degrees for 10 minutes. Cut in half and insert ham slices.

BLUEBERRY CAKE

1 cup plain flour
¼ cup brown sugar
1 stick butter or margarine, softened
1 cup chopped pecans

In a large mixing bowl, mix all ingredients, using a potato masher. When well-blended, pat mixture into an ungreased 9 × 12-inch baking pan. Bake at 350 degrees until brown on top. Cool.

Filling
2½ cups blueberries
1 cup sugar
¼ cup plain flour
1 tablespoon lemon juice

In a medium saucepan, combine ingredients and simmer over low heat until thickened. Cool.

Topping
1 cup whipping cream
6 ounces cream cheese, room temperature
¾ cup sugar
1 teaspoon vanilla

In a large mixing bowl, beat cream until it forms a soft peak. Add cream cheese, sugar, and vanilla and continue to beat until well blended.

To assemble, place cake on a large platter. Spread with filling. Top with whipped cream mixture. Chill and cut into squares for serving.

FRUIT SALAD

Sarah says this fruit salad dates back over one hundred years. The original recipe calls for a 10-cent bottle of cherries and a 10-cent package of marshmallows.

12 large marshmallows
1 8-ounce can fruit cocktail and juice
1 pint cream, whipped

2 to 3 bananas, peeled and sliced
1 large can crushed pineapple, drained
1 6-ounce jar maraschino cherries

In a medium saucepan, combine marshmallows and
fruit juice. Warm over low heat until marshmallows
melt into fruit juice. Remove from heat and stir in
whipped cream and remaining ingredients. Combine
well. Pour mixture into a 9 × 12-inch dish. Freeze.
To serve, cut into squares.

MOLASSES PIE

¾ cup sugar
1 tablespoon butter, softened
3 eggs
1 cup milk
¾ cup dark molasses
1 tablespoon plain flour
1 9-inch pie shell

Combine sugar, butter, eggs, milk, molasses, and
flour in a large mixing bowl. Mix well. Pour into a
9-inch unbaked pie shell. Bake at 425 degrees for
10 minutes and lower heat to 400 degrees. Bake until
set.

PULL CANDY

1½ cups sugar
½ cup vinegar

In a medium saucepan, combine sugar and vinegar.
Bring to a boil and cook to the hard ball stage
(275 degrees on a candy thermometer or until a drop
of the mixture forms a hard ball when dropped into
water). Pour mixture onto a marble slab or other
hard surface and cool until you can handle it. Pull

candy with hands until it becomes cream colored and stiff. Crack into pieces with the back of a knife. Store in an airtight container.

DROP DOUGHNUTS

1 cup milk
1 cup sugar
1 egg
3 cups plain flour
½ teaspoon ground nutmeg
2 teaspoons baking powder
½ teaspoon salt
vegetable oil
½ cup sugar

In a large mixing bowl, combine milk, sugar, and egg. Mix well. Sift together flour, nutmeg, baking powder, and salt. Slowly add flour mixture to liquid. Combine well. Place about 4 inches of cooking oil in a large saucepan or deep-fat fryer. Using hands, drop small balls of dough into the hot oil. When doughnuts are golden brown, remove from the oil and drain on paper towels. Roll doughnuts in sugar.

BROWN SUGAR CHEWY CAKE

Sarah says this cake will look like it is still not done when you pull it out of the oven after fifteen minutes. But when you taste it, you will change your mind.

1 pound brown sugar
1 stick butter or margarine
3 eggs
2 cups self-rising flour
1 cup nuts
1 teaspoon vanilla
½ teaspoon cinnamon

Melt together sugar and butter in a medium saucepan over medium heat. Allow to cool slightly. Add remaining ingredients and combine thoroughly. Pour

70

into a 9 × 12-inch pan and bake at 375 degrees for
15 minutes.

FUDGE

2 cups sugar
2 heaping tablespoons corn syrup
½ cup milk
4 tablespoons cocoa
2 tablespoons butter

In a medium saucepan, combine sugar, corn syrup,
milk, and cocoa. Bring to a boil and cook to the
hard ball stage (275 degrees on a candy thermometer or until a drop of the mixture forms a hard ball
when dropped into water). Add butter and combine
well. Pour into a shallow 9 × 9-inch baking dish to
harden.

VENICE WILLIAMS
Avon

What's it like living through a hurricane at Avon?" you ask Venice Williams. She replies in two words—"Quite exciting."

Venice remembers the "big storm" of 1944. That was before hurricanes had names. The ocean and sound waters met at Venice's house in Avon. Her family moved to a neighbor's house on higher ground. But even then, the first floor of that house filled with water.

Venice and her family returned home to find that their house was not where they had left it. "Houses were off their blocks and over the beach a ways," she says. A few minutes of searching turned up her family's house intact, but on the beach nearly a mile away.

Those were the days when the quickest way off the island was a ferry to the mainland. But even then, most folks chose to ride out a storm. Hurricane tracking was not as sophisticated as it is today, and no one had even heard of a hurricane shelter. When a storm was headed in its direction, the community pulled together. They battened down as best they could and then waited it out.

Through storm and calm, Avon has been home to Venice all her life. Her husband is a commercial fisherman, and seafood has always been a big part of the Williams menu. "I like seafood any way you fix it," says Venice. Her advice on choosing fish: drum is best in the spring and fall, spot in the summer, and speckled and gray trout any time of year. Oysters, she adds, are best avoided in the summer because they get milky and tasteless.

FRIED SPOT

¾ cup cornmeal
1 teaspoon salt
½ teaspoon black pepper
4 pounds spot, dressed with heads on
¾ cup vegetable oil

In a mixing bowl, combine dry ingredients. Dredge
spot in cornmeal mixture. In a large skillet, panfry
spot in oil over medium high heat. Brown both
sides. Serves 4.

STEWED PORK CHOPS AND PORK LIVER WITH DUMPLINGS AND PASTRY

Venice uses this same recipe, with the addition of diced Irish potatoes and onions, for stewing crabs, chicken, pork chops, and spareribs.

2 thin slices salt pork
1 pound pork liver
1 pound pork chops
water
cornmeal dumplings (recipes, pp. 104, 116, and 138)
pastry (see recipe below)

In a medium saucepan, render fat from salt pork. Remove meat. Slice liver into pieces. Place liver and
pork chops in saucepan. Add enough water to cover
about 1 inch above the meat. Bring to a boil, reduce
heat and simmer 1 hour. Add cornmeal dumplings
and then top with pastry strips and simmer 30 minutes. Serves 8.

Pastry
2 cups plain flour
½ teaspoon salt
1 tablespoon shortening
⅔ cup water

Sift together flour and salt. Cut in shortening. Add water and work dough into a soft ball. Let dough stand for 10 minutes. Using a rolling pin, roll dough flat and cut into strips, 1 × 3 inches.

FRIED CHICKEN

1 chicken, cut up
1 teaspoon salt
½ teaspoon black pepper
¾ cup pancake flour
¾ cup shortening

Sprinkle chicken pieces with salt and pepper. Dredge in pancake flour. In a large skillet, melt shortening. Panfry chicken slowly over medium low heat about 30 minutes on each side. Serves 4.

Venice says corn pone bread is good with roast beef and gravy or fried chicken.

CORN PONE BREAD

2 cups white cornmeal
½ cup plain flour
1 quart boiling water
¼ teaspoon baking soda
½ cup sugar
½ cup molasses
1 teaspoon salt
2 tablespoons shortening

Place meal and flour in a large mixing bowl. Stir in hot water. Cover and let stand overnight. The next morning, add baking soda, sugar, molasses, and salt and stir. On the stove, melt shortening in a deep iron skillet. Pour in mixture and place skillet in a 350-degree oven. Bake for 1½ hours. Slice and serve.

COCONUT PIE

1 5-ounce can evaporated milk
½ cup water
3 eggs, beaten
1 tablespoon cornstarch
1 cup coconut
1½ cups sugar
½ stick butter or margarine, melted
1 deep-dish 9-inch pie shell, unbaked

Mix together milk, water, eggs, cornstarch, coconut, sugar, and butter or margarine. Pour into unbaked pie shell. Bake at 350 degrees 40 to 45 minutes or until firm when shaken.

BLACKBERRY SPREAD

1 quart blackberries, washed
2 cups sugar
¼ cup water
2 tablespoons cornstarch

Place berries in a large saucepan on the stove. Add sugar and water. Simmer on low heat until berries fall apart. Add cornstarch to thicken.

Venice eats her blackberry spread with a biscuit, or she prepares a pie with the same mixture. For pie, she pours the spread into a baked pie shell and tops with whipped cream.

EVELYN STYRON
Hatteras

Before the bridge over Oregon Inlet connected Hatteras Island to the rest of the state, supplies came by boat from Elizabeth City or Washington. Once the bridge was built in the 1960s, her village changed, says Evelyn Styron. "It's certainly more convenient now, but there are bad points, too. There was more togetherness before the bridge. I used to know everybody on the island— their names and ancestry."

Evelyn's resume includes over thirty years of restaurant cooking. She laments the way seafood is cooked in restaurants these days. "Seafood doesn't need to be so heavily breaded. Shrimp are dipped and dipped again until you have more batter than shrimp."

The people on the island are different, too, she adds. In the days before the bridge, the islanders were self-sufficient. "We're getting to be a lazy people today. We depend too much on grocery stores," she says.

Pamlico Sound backs up to Evelyn's house in Hatteras Village. Her husband used to set out stake nets each morning and bring in fish for breakfast. "There's nothing better than hot biscuits or grits with fried fish for breakfast," she says.

Evelyn says you will find sea trout at the fish market in the summer and speckled trout in the winter. Both are favorites of Hatteras natives.

FRIED TROUT

½ cup plain flour
½ cup white cornmeal
1 teaspoon salt
¼ teaspoon black pepper
2 pounds trout fillets
½ cup shortening or vegetable oil

In a mixing bowl, combine flour, cornmeal, salt, and pepper. Dredge fillets in seasoned flour and cornmeal. In a large frying pan, fry fillets in shortening or oil over medium high heat until fish is golden brown on both sides. Serves 4.

BROILED TROUT

2 tablespoons vegetable oil or margarine
2 pounds trout fillets
¼ teaspoon paprika

Using your hands, rub oil or margarine on fillets. Sprinkle with paprika. In a casserole, broil fillets until meat flakes. Serves 4.

STEWED GOOSE

1 6- to 10-pound goose, cleaned and
   cut into pieces like a chicken
2 teaspoons salt
1 teaspoon black pepper
water
1 rutabaga, peeled and cut into chunks
2 tablespoons plain flour
½ cup water

Place goose in a large roasting pan. Salt and pepper. Nearly cover with water. Cover pan and simmer on medium heat for 3½ hours. Add rutabaga and simmer 1½ hours more. Remove goose and rutabaga ` from broth. In a jar, add flour and ½ cup water and shake vigorously. Add to broth to thicken for gravy. Serve gravy in a separate bowl. Serves 6 to 8.

Evelyn likes her salad moist; so she uses a lot of mayonnaise and mustard. If you prefer a drier potato salad, cut down on the mayonnaise and mustard.

POTATO SALAD

6 medium Irish potatoes, peeled and diced
water
2 teaspoons salt
1 small onion, diced
2 hard-boiled eggs, chopped
1 stalk celery, chopped, or 1 teaspoon celery seed
1 bell pepper, finely diced (optional)
¾ cup mayonnaise
2 tablespoons prepared mustard
¼ cup sweet pickle relish
¼ teaspoon black pepper
1 teaspoon sugar

In a large pot, cover potatoes with water. Salt. Boil potatoes until tender and drain. In a large mixing bowl, combine hot potatoes, onion, eggs, celery, and bell pepper. Add mayonnaise, mustard, and relish. Combine. Season with pepper and sugar. Serves 6 to 8.

COLE SLAW

Evelyn uses sweet pickle relish instead of vinegar to flavor her cole slaw, and she recommends a dash of salt to kill the flatness of the cabbage. A unique ingredient—a cubed apple—gives Evelyn's slaw a taste of its own.

1 medium-sized cabbage, grated
1 small onion, finely diced
1 apple, finely cubed
1 tablespoon sweet pickle relish and juice
½ cup mayonnaise
1 heaping tablespoon sugar
¼ teaspoon salt
1 teaspoon celery seed

In a large mixing bowl, combine cabbage, onion, and apple. Add relish, mayonnaise, sugar, and seasonings. Combine. Serves 6 to 8.

FIG PUDDING

2 quarts steamed figs
2 tablespoons butter
2 cups sugar
1 egg, beaten
1½ cups plain flour
¼ teaspoon ground nutmeg
½ teaspoon cinnamon
1 teaspoon vanilla (optional)

With a knife and fork, chop figs, adding butter. Add sugar, egg, flour, spices, and vanilla to figs. Combine. Butter a 9 × 12-inch baking pan. Pour in mixture and bake 30 minutes at 350 to 400 degrees until firm.

PUMPKIN PIE

2 cups fresh pumpkin pulp, cooked and mashed
    (or 1 can of pumpkin)
3 eggs, beaten
1½ cups sugar
¾ cup evaporated milk
¼ teaspoon salt
1 teaspoon cinnamon
1 teaspoon ground nutmeg
1 9-inch unbaked pie crust (see below)

In a mixing bowl, combine pumpkin, eggs, sugar, milk, salt, cinnamon, and nutmeg. Mix well. Pour into pie crust. Bake for 45 minutes at 375 degrees or until pie is firm when shaken.

Pie crust
2 cups plain flour
½ teaspoon salt
¾ cup shortening
¼ cup water

Sift flour and salt into mixing bowl. Cut shortening into flour mixture until it resembles cornmeal. Sprinkle with water. With hands, work dough until well blended. On a floured surface, roll dough to a ⅛-inch thickness using a rolling pin. Lift dough from surface and press into a 9-inch pie pan. With a knife, cut excess from edges.

ELIZABETH HOWARD
Ocracoke

Seventy-five-year-old Elizabeth Howard is a native Ocracoker. Born and raised on this remote island, Elizabeth has memories of Ocracoke that hold spellbound those newly initiated to this island's unique culture.

"People used to come up to the natives and ask if we had much to eat here," she says. Her reply: "You name it and we ate it"—including sea turtle. Before sea turtles were placed on the wildlife endangered and threatened species list, many residents such as Elizabeth prepared and ate the large loggerhead turtle. She used the legs of the turtle to make a stew with potatoes and cornmeal dumplings. But since the large reptiles have become protected by law, Elizabeth can no longer include this dish on her menus.

Elizabeth also remembers when commercial fishing was the mainstay of existence on the island. The natives feasted on the ocean's bounty—drum, crabs, mackerel, and spot. What fish they didn't eat, they salted in barrels and sold to northern markets. Or they bartered their catch with inland Hyde County farmers for fresh vegetables.

Most Ocracoke families were like Elizabeth's. They grew their own vegetables and kept cows, pigs, sheep, and horses. Some horses roamed free until the highway was built in 1957. Most of the homes were surrounded by fences that kept these roaming herds of horses away from the house. "Ocracoke is the only place I know where the people were fenced in and the animals roamed free," remarked one islander.

Fish was not the only bounty the sea gave Ocracoke. Occasionally the treacherous shoals off Ocracoke would waylay a passing vessel, leaving the spoils for the islanders. Many island homes, including Elizabeth's, were built from lumber those ships were carrying to the West Indies.

Every coastal village has a story about the "worst hurricane," and Ocracoke is no exception. Elizabeth says the worst storm of her lifetime came in 1944, the hurricane Elizabeth calls "The Great Atlantic." "I was shelling shrimp when I noticed the water coming in the yard," she says. "It kept coming and coming. Finally the sound and the sea met. There was 12 inches of water in this house. Fish washed into some houses and trawlers were pushed onto land."

Today, Elizabeth's recollections of an earlier Ocracoke bring a smile to her face. She remembers when all island babies were brought into the world by midwives, when Silver Lake was called Cockle Creek, and when the only way off the island was a mailboat to Atlantic or an occasional steamer to Washington.

Elizabeth says puppy drum is what islanders call a small channel bass.

PUPPY DRUM (CHANNEL BASS) AND POTATOES

1 4- to 6-pound drum, filleted
1 teaspoon salt
6 medium Irish potatoes, peeled and diced
2 slices salt pork, diced
1 to 2 medium onions, diced
2 hard-boiled eggs, sliced

In a large saucepan, cover fillets with water. Add salt and boil until fish flakes. In a smaller saucepan, boil potatoes until tender. Panfry salt pork until meat is crisp (cracklings).

Take up fish in one dish, potatoes in another. On a plate, mix fish and potatoes with a fork. Sprinkle raw onions over mixture and top with meat grease and cracklings. Top with slices of hard-boiled egg.
Serves 4 to 6.

BAKED LEG OF LAMB

1 to 2 cloves garlic, crushed
1 leg of lamb, 5 to 6 pounds
1 teaspoon salt
½ teaspoon black pepper
2 cups water
1 to 2 onions, sliced

Rub garlic over lamb leg. Salt and pepper. Place in an uncovered roasting pan in a 350-degree oven. Roast for 30 minutes or until brown. Add water to the roasting pan and cover. Roast for 2½ hours. Add sliced onions midway through cooking time. Serves 8 to 10.

BLACKBERRY OR APPLE DUMPLINGS

2 cups sifted plain flour
2 heaping teaspoons baking powder
½ teaspoon salt
2 tablespoons margarine or shortening
⅓ to ½ cup cold water
1 quart fresh blackberries or sliced apples
sauce (see recipe below)

In a mixing bowl, combine flour, baking powder and salt. Cut in margarine or shortening. Add enough cold water to hold the mixture together. Work into dough.

Pinch off a small ball of dough. Handling lightly, roll into a 6-inch circle with a rolling pin. Place about ¼ cup berries or apples in the center of the dough. Draw all sides of the dough together (like a drawstring purse) and pinch to close.

Drop 2 to 3 dumplings at a time into a large saucepan of gently boiling water. Simmer 15 to

Elizabeth says her father, brother, and nephew gathered around the table just before she pulled the dumplings from the pot. "They could eat four apiece," she says.

SUGAR

Colonial America was not a place for those with a sweet tooth. In the 1700s, sugar was expensive. For those who could afford its sweetness, sugar was bought in cones and shaved off as it was needed. In fact, this sweetener was so precious many people kept it locked away. In the South, molasses was a frequent sugar substitute. But even with the availability of molasses, many fruit desserts went unsweetened. As the availability of sugar increased, many cooks added sugary sauces to sweeten these desserts.

20 minutes until the dough is tough and not sticky. When the dumplings are done, remove them from the pot with a slotted spoon. Pour sauce over the hot dumplings just before serving. Makes 16 to 20 dumplings.

Sauce

4 eggs, separated
1 cup plus 3 tablespoons sugar
1 teaspoon vanilla
½ teaspoon ground nutmeg
1 cup whipping cream

In a mixing bowl, beat the egg yolks until lemon-colored. Gradually add 1 cup of sugar until the mixture is stiff. Add vanilla and nutmeg. In another bowl, beat egg whites and 2 tablespoons of sugar until stiff. In a third bowl, beat the whipping cream and 1 tablespoon of sugar until stiff. Just before the dumplings are done, fold together yolks, whites, and whipped cream.

JELLY CAKE

Elizabeth concocted the filling for this cake when she was a young girl. She pulled the ingredients from the shelves of her father's store on Ocracoke.

½ pound butter, room temperature
2 cups sugar
4 eggs
3 cups plain flour
3 heaping teaspoons baking powder
1 cup milk
1 teaspoon vanilla
filling (see recipe below)

In a mixing bowl, cream butter and sugar until fluffy. Add eggs one at a time; mix thoroughly. Sift together flour and baking powder. Add flour and milk alternately. Stir in vanilla. Pour into four 8-inch greased and floured cake pans. Bake at 350 degrees for 30 to 40 minutes.

Filling and topping
1 8-ounce can cranberry sauce
½ 10-ounce jar grape jelly
½ 10-ounce jar guava jelly

In a mixing bowl, mix sauce and jellies with a beater until smooth. Spread between layers and on top of cake.

CHOCOLATE CAKE

Using the preceding cake batter recipe, make cake layers or a sheet cake. Use the following icing as a topping and between layers.

2 cups sugar
3 rounded tablespoons cocoa
1 cup milk
3 tablespoons butter
½ teaspoon salt

In a saucepan, mix sugar and cocoa. Add milk. Place on stove and bring to a boil. Add butter and salt. Turn temperature to low and cook slowly until the chocolate mixture reaches the soft ball stage on the candy thermometer or until a small amount of the mixture dropped into cold water can be formed into a soft ball. If the icing becomes hard, add extra butter or milk.

LUCILLE TRUITT
Oriental

Lucille Truitt is a fisherman. She can smell a school of fish on the air and read the weather in the sky. She talks of mullet fishing and painting the thing she knows best—the Neuse River.

Born at Paw Cats Creek in Goosetail Swamp, Lucille says, "Fishing was born into me. I spent the first six years of my life on the river [Neuse]. We lived on an old flat my father pulled up and down the river. He fished for shad, and my mother dried the fish and picked the fatbacks.

"My father and generations back—to the Vikings—were fishermen. It must be in my blood, and I can't swim a lick."

But Lucille's inability to swim does not stop her from taking to the water. All her husband Billy has to do is mention shrimping, crabbing, or fishing, and Lucille is ready to close the door on the couple's junk shop in Oriental. She fishes alongside Billy on their 30-foot boat, the *Sea Hound*. "I work like a man," she says. "But he treats me like a woman."

Although Lucille likes to fish for about anything the nets drag up, she has taken a particular liking to mullet. "Mullet fishing is the best sport in the world," she says. "Billy and I go out on dark nights. We pole along real quiet and listen for the fish washing themselves. When we find a school, we set the net. Then we turn on the light and start hollering, banging the side of the boat, and slapping the water. Boy, the mullet start flying. They're coming in the boat, over the boat. Billy always tells me to duck, but I don't like to miss a single minute."

Lucille may be first mate on the water, but in the kitchen she is captain. She cooks many of the same dishes her mother did—old drum stew, fried mullet, and collards. In fact, there are often people who just happen by the store at mealtime hoping for a chance to sit down at Lucille's table.

Lucille says there are
three types of drum:
puppy drum, yearling,
and old drum. Using her
hands, she shows that a
puppy drum measures
about 10 to 12 inches in
length, a yearling about
18 to 20 inches, and
an old drum 28 to 30
inches. Lucille prefers
old drum for her stew.
To clean the large fish,
she "nails their tails to a
board and scales 'em
with a hoe."

OLD DRUM STEW

4 medium Irish potatoes, quartered
water
2 pounds old drum fillets
¼ pound salt pork
1 medium onion, diced
cornmeal dumplings (recipes, pp. 104, 116, and 138)

In a large saucepan, place quartered potatoes and
cover with water. Bring to a boil, reduce heat, and
simmer for 20 minutes. Meanwhile cut drum fillets
into chunks. In a skillet, render fat from salt pork.
Remove meat and save drippings. Over potatoes,
add a layer of diced onions and then a layer of
chunked drum. Pour pork drippings over stew. Shake
saucepan gently from side to side to mix ingredients.
Continue simmering 30 to 45 minutes or until broth
thickens. Add cornmeal dumplings and simmer 10
more minutes. Serves 6 to 8.

*Mullet is Lucille's favor-
ite fish. "I guess I like
them because I love to
catch them so much,"
she says. "I fry the ones
we catch between the
ole lighthouse and here.
I wouldn't give a nickel
for a mullet after they
pass the lighthouse." Lu-
cille explains that mullet
caught over a sandy bot-
tom have a better flavor.
They don't have the
muddy, musty flavor
characteristic of mullet
caught over a muddy
bottom, she says.*

FRIED MULLET

1½ pounds mullet fillets
1 cup cornmeal
½ teaspoon salt
¾ cup vegetable oil

Dredge fillets in cornmeal. Salt lightly. Panfry in oil
over medium high heat on both sides until golden
brown. Serves 4.

BROILED SPANISH MACKEREL

1½ pounds Spanish mackerel fillets
½ teaspoon salt
3 tablespoons butter

Place fillets, skin side up, in a greased baking dish. Place under broiler. Broil until slightly brown. Remove from broiler, turn fillets and salt. Slice butter and place over fillets. Return to broiler. Broil until slightly brown and fish flakes. Serves 4.

VENISON HAM

2 teaspoons salt
1 teaspoon black pepper
¾ cup plain flour
1 8- to 10-pound venison ham
½ cup vegetable oil
1 bell pepper, sliced
2 onions, sliced
1 tablespoon Worcestershire sauce
1 cup red wine
2 cups water

Preheat oven to 450 degrees. Salt, pepper, and flour venison. Place oil in a large roasting pan and heat in oven. When pan is hot, add ham and sear all sides. Remove from oven. Reduce oven temperature to 300 degrees. Add remaining ingredients and cover pan. Place in oven. Roast 20 minutes per pound of meat. Baste frequently.

COLLARDS AND IRISH POTATOES

2 pounds collards, washed
½ gallon water
½ pound salt pork, sliced
5 medium Irish potatoes, quartered
cornmeal dumplings (recipes, pp. 104, 116, and 138)

Cut up collards. In a 4- to 6-quart pot, add water and salt pork. Bring to a boil, reduce heat. Add collards.

Lucille says that the amount of time needed to cook collards depends on the time of the year. They cook faster in the summer, she says. She also washes her collards three times. That way she can rid the leafy vegetables of sand, grit, and collard worms.

89

Simmer 2 hours. More water may be needed. Add potatoes. Simmer 50 minutes. Add cornmeal dumplings. Simmer 10 minutes longer. Serves 4.

CHOCOLATE CAKE

When Lucille assembles her cake, she punches several holes in each layer with a spoon. This allows the icing to seep through the cake. Lucille admits the finished product is not pretty because the holes make the cake crater, but her family does not complain. They can eat a whole cake in one day.

1 cup butter, room temperature
2 cups sugar
4 eggs
3 cups self-rising flour
1 cup water
icing (see recipe below)

In a mixing bowl, cream butter and sugar. Add eggs one at a time. Add flour and water alternately. Divide batter among 4 greased and floured 8-inch cake pans. Bake at 350 degrees for 25 to 30 minutes or until a knife inserted in the cake comes out clean. Remove from oven. Cool 5 minutes, then turn layers out onto a cake rack. Cool completely and ice.

Icing
3 cups sugar
⅔ cup cocoa
⅛ teaspoon salt
1 14-ounce can evaporated milk

In a medium saucepan, combine sugar, cocoa, and salt. Stir in milk. Bring to a boil over medium heat, stirring constantly. Boil 5 minutes. Remove from heat; cool.

GLENNIE WILLIS
Atlantic

G lennie Willis's family goes way back. She proudly proclaims that they were some of the original "Downeasters." And of course being a Downeaster means she has a natural affinity for stews, pastry, cornmeal dumplings, and seafood.

In the kitchen, Glennie uses her hands and fingers to dip up flour and scoop out shortening. So when she first tells you the ingredients for her recipes, she says a handful of this, a dip of that, a pinch of this, or a nickit of that. But if she thinks about it a few minutes, Glennie can translate into the more conventional quarts, cups, and tablespoons.

Glennie has a particular fondness for wild meat—game and waterfowl. Back when wild game was plentiful, she would rather have served up venison stew or wild duck than pork or chicken.

Coming from a long line of watermen and boat-builders, Glennie knows her seafood. She says that fish caught in the early spring and fall are tastier than fish caught at other times of the year. And she claims that there is no better eating fish caught anywhere than in the inlet at Hatteras. Fish taken from moving waters are always better, she says.

And why not eat oysters during "non-R" months (May, June, July, and August)? "They spawn during those months," Glennie says, which makes the bivalves watery and not as flavorful.

FRIED SCALLOPS

½ cup shortening
1 large egg
1 pound bay scallops
paper bag
¾ cup plain flour

Glennie flours her scallops by placing them, with flour and seasonings, in a paper bag and shaking the bag vigorously. She believes this method provides a more thorough and even coating.

SCALLOPS

Three types of scallops are harvested along the East Coast, but only two—the calico and bay—are native to North Carolina waters. The larger Atlantic deep-sea scallop is harvested in New England. The most abundant Tar Heel scallop, the bay, is harvested, as its name indicates, from estuarine waters. The calico is an offshore scallop that periodically and somewhat mysteriously appears in a large bed off Carteret County. Both the calico and the bay are proclaimed by many to be sweeter and more tender than their northern cousins.

Unlike the clam and oyster, all of the scallop's soft body is not eaten. Only the adductor muscle is food for the table.

½ teaspoon salt
¼ teaspoon black pepper

Melt shortening in a skillet over medium high heat. In a mixing bowl, break an egg over scallops and mix thoroughly. In a paper bag, combine flour, salt, and pepper. Add scallops to bag. Shake vigorously. Drop the scallops, one by one, into hot shortening. Cook until golden brown on all sides. Serves 4.

STEWED OYSTERS

In the old days, Glennie says, when oysters were plentiful, people in Atlantic made their oyster stew out of oysters, butter, and, of course, a topping of cornmeal dumplings. But today oysters are not so abundant, and Glennie says many folks stretch the oysters by adding water or milk. But she never adds milk. And she says you must be careful not to overcook the oysters or they will become tough.

1½ quarts shucked oysters and juices
¼ cup butter
cornmeal dumplings (recipes, pp. 104, 116, and 138)

To a large saucepan, add oysters, their juices, and butter. Bring to a boil. Reduce oysters to a simmer and add cornmeal dumplings. Simmer 20 minutes. Serves 4 to 6.

DEVILED CRAB CASSEROLE

1 medium onion, diced
1 small stalk celery, diced
1 green bell pepper or red bell pepper, chopped
2 tablespoons butter
1 pound cooked crab meat, preferably claw meat
4 slices bread, toasted until brown
1 cup milk
1 cup mayonnaise
3 tablespoons catsup
1 teaspoon mustard
⅛ teaspoon cumin
½ teaspoon salt
¼ teaspoon black pepper
paprika
small pats of butter

In a skillet, sauté onion, celery, and bell pepper in
butter. In a mixing bowl, add sautéed vegetables to
crab meat. Crumble toast and add to crab meat. Pour
in milk. Add mayonnaise, catsup, mustard, cumin,
salt, and pepper. Mix thoroughly. Spread the crab
mixture in a 9 × 12-inch baking pan. Sprinkle with
paprika. Add small pats of butter to the top of the
casserole. Bake at 350 degrees for 35 minutes.
Serves 4 to 6.

*Glennie recommends a
particular brand of may-
onnaise for her crab
casserole. And she won't
hear of any other kind.
"You can't build a good
house with bad lumber,
so use Hellman's may-
onnaise," she says.*

FISH HASH

4 2- to 4-pound Spanish mackerel, in the round
1 26-ounce box table salt
1 to 2 thin slices salt pork
2 quarts water
3 medium Irish potatoes, diced
2 medium onions, diced
1 teaspoon salt
½ teaspoon black pepper

*Glennie says you should
begin this recipe three to
four days prior to
serving.*

Eviscerate Spanish mackerel and remove head and backbone. Place in a glass baking dish. Pack with salt, being sure to rub salt inside cavity of the fish. Let stand for 3 days in the refrigerator. Remove from salt and wash. Pull skin from fish. Soak in fresh water in the refrigerator for 4 to 6 hours, changing water several times. Chunk fish.

In a saucepan, render fat from salt pork. Remove meat. Add chunked mackerel, water, potatoes, onions, salt, and pepper. Simmer until potatoes are tender. Remove from heat and drain. Mince fish, potatoes, and onions into a hash. Serves 4 to 8.

SPOT AND SWEET POTATOES

As with the fish hash, Glennie begins this recipe four days prior to its serving. To appreciate this dish fully, she recommends alternating bites of fish and baked sweet potato.

4 spot, in the round
1 26-ounce box table salt
4 sweet potatoes
water
white vinegar

Gut, scale, and remove backbone from fish. Place in a large pan and pack with salt, being sure to rub flesh and inner cavity of fish with salt. Place in the refrigerator for 4 days.

To cook, remove fish from salt and wash. Soak in fresh water 4 to 6 hours in the refrigerator, changing water several times. Place in a large saucepan and cover with water. Bring to a boil, reduce heat and simmer until fish is tender and flaky. Meanwhile bake sweet potatoes until tender. Remove fish from saucepan, placing one on each serving plate. Sprinkle with vinegar. Serve with sweet potatoes. Serves 4.

STEWED DIAMONDBACK TERRAPIN

legs from 3 to 4 diamondback terrapins
1 quart boiling water
1 to 2 thin slices salt pork
1 quart water
3 medium Irish potatoes, diced
2 medium onions, finely diced
salt to taste
black pepper to taste

Scald terrapin legs with boiling water and remove skin. Trim away fat. Cut meat into chunks or divide into quarters. In a large saucepan, render fat from salt pork. Remove meat. Add terrapin, water, potatoes, onions, salt, and pepper. Bring to a boil, reduce heat, and simmer until meat is tender, about 2 hours. Serves 4.

STEWED VENISON

2 to 3 thin slices salt pork
1 tablespoon plain flour
2 pounds venison, cut into strips or chunks
1 to 2 quarts water
1 medium onion, sliced
½ teaspoon salt
½ teaspoon black pepper

In a large saucepan, render fat from salt pork. Remove meat. Brown flour in grease. Add venison and cover with water. Add sliced onion, salt, and pepper. Stir. Simmer until tender, about 2 hours. Serves 4.

DIAMONDBACK TERRAPIN

During the Gay Nineties the diamondback terrapin made a name for itself on the menus of America's finest restaurants. It was stirred into a soup praised by gourmets.

To keep the restaurants stocked with meat, hunters killed thousands of the reptiles in tidal marshes from Maryland to Georgia. In fact, so many diamondback terrapins were killed that their populations dwindled and prices reached as high as $120 a dozen during the 1890s.

Political pressure was placed on the federal government to solve the problem of the terrapin's short supply. The solution was a hatchery.

Since North Carolina was central to the reptile's distribution, it was decided to locate the hatchery on Pivers Island near Beaufort at the new U.S. Fishery Laboratory. But fishery personnel soon found that hatching eggs and raising terrapins from a wild brood stock was not like raising chickens.

Over ten years of effort ensued before the first young terrapins were released into the wild in 1913. But the hatchery continued to meet with success, and by the late 1920s more than a quarter of a million young terrapins had been released in salt marshes from Maryland to Florida.

By then, however, the terrapin soup fad had faded. With the pressure of hunting removed, diamond terrapin populations again flourished, possibly aided by the influx of hatchery young.

STEWED RUTABAGAS

2 medium rutabagas, peeled and sliced
2 to 3 slices salt pork
1 to 1½ quarts water
½ teaspoon sugar

In a saucepan, render the fat from salt pork. Remove meat. Add rutabagas to the saucepan and cover with water. Add sugar. Simmer until rutabagas are tender. Serves 4.

"Rutabagas are a very good winter vegetable down our way," Glennie says. "We often put it in beef, duck, and pork stews."

MITCHELL AND VILMA MORRIS
Smyrna

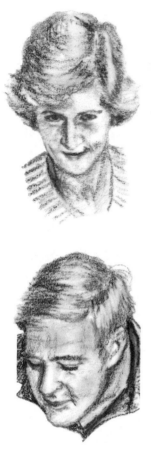

Mitchell Morris received his initiation as a cook when he was thirteen years old. He stumbled onto a 36-foot commercial fishing boat at 3:30 one morning, ready to begin his career. The response to his arrival was none too welcoming. A big, burly captain, fists on his hips, looked down at little Mitchell and demanded, "Boy, you ever cooked before?" And, without waiting for an answer, added, "I want to see flour to your elbows every morning because I want hot biscuits three times a day."

Mitchell never got a chance to tell the captain that if the truth were known, he had never cooked a day in his life. Today, he laughs and admits that after his first batch of biscuits, the captain probably had his answer to that first question. Mitchell says those biscuits would have killed a bull.

But somehow, Mitchell managed to keep the crew well nourished. When the boat would stay on the water several weeks at a time, the crew ate fish every day, he says. In the evenings, they would anchor near Portsmouth and go ashore to hunt for birds to add a little variety to their meals. Mitchell would stew fry just about any bird they could kill—graybacks, sea robins, yellow sharks, black ducks, and mallards.

A favorite seafood meal in the winter was salted spot, boiled for breakfast and served with fried corn bread and baked sweet potatoes. Mitchell says a little hot vinegar poured over the fish could really take the bite out of a cold morning on the water.

These days Mitchell and his wife, Vilma, live in Smyrna, and they catch most of their own seafood. A true Downeaster, they say, only eats seafood that is in season. Vilma motions toward the water and says, "We call that our supermarket."

Now Vilma does most of the cooking in the Morris kitchen. But Mitchell takes full credit for her tasty creations. He says he taught his wife everything she knows about cooking—except maybe how to make biscuits. "None of those nylon biscuits for us," says Mitchell, describing the pop-open biscuits available on the store shelves.

STEW-FRIED SHRIMP

2 to 3 thin slices salt pork
1 pound cooked shrimp, headed, peeled, and deveined
¼ cup plain flour
4 cups water
1 teaspoon salt
½ teaspoon black pepper
½ cup rice, uncooked (optional)

Render fat from salt pork in an iron skillet. Remove meat. Add shrimp and panfry over medium heat 5 minutes. Add flour and stir. Add water, salt, and pepper. Simmer 20 minutes, stirring constantly. If rice is desired, add 15 minutes before serving. Serves 4.

Vilma often uses leftover steamed shrimp from the preceding day for her stew-fried shrimp. To make her leftovers go a little further, she makes a gravy. If unexpected guests drop by, she adds rice to the stew about fifteen minutes before it is done to stretch the dish even further.

OYSTER STEW

1 pint shucked oysters and juices
water
1 teaspoon salt
½ teaspoon black pepper
cornmeal dumplings (recipes, pp. 104, 116, and 138)

Place oysters and juices in a large saucepan. Add water 1½ inches above oysters. Salt and pepper. Sim-

Mitchell says the oysters harvested near Portsmouth Island are far superior to any found along the East Coast, even the highly touted Chesapeake Bay oyster. And Mitchell insists that no milk be added to his stew. If cooked long enough, the oyster's own natural juices will turn a milky white.

mer 2 hours (additional water may be needed). Add cornmeal dumplings and simmer an additional hour. Serves 4.

OYSTER FRITTERS

Vilma says the amount of salt needed to season the fritters will vary because some oysters are saltier than others.

1 pint shucked oysters, whole, and juices
1 cup self-rising flour
salt to taste
½ teaspoon black pepper
½ cup vegetable oil

In a mixing bowl, combine oysters and juices, flour, salt, and pepper. Mix until oysters are evenly coated. Drop by large spoonfuls into 1 inch of hot oil in a skillet. Panfry on both sides until golden brown. Serves 4.

STEW-FRIED BIRDS*

Mitchell has stew-fried graybacks, sea robins, yellow sharks, mallards, and black ducks. He used only the breasts and thighs because, he says, the backs gave the stew a bad flavor.

8 bird or duck breasts and thighs, cleaned
water
2 to 3 thin slices salt pork
¼ cup plain flour
4 cups water
1 teaspoon salt
½ teaspoon black pepper

*Before shooting any of the birds mentioned in the above recipe, check with a wildlife officer for information on hunting seasons. Also be sure that none of the birds is listed on the threatened or endangered lists.

Place bird breasts and thighs in a large saucepan; cover with water. Parboil 30 minutes. Remove meat from saucepan and cool. Pull meat from bone and tear into bite-size pieces. In a skillet, render fat from salt pork and remove pork meat. Add breasts and thighs and panfry 2 to 3 minutes. Meanwhile, in a jar, add flour to one cup of water, shaking vigorously until thoroughly mixed. Add to skillet. Add remaining water, salt, and pepper. Simmer 20 minutes, stirring constantly. Serves 4.

SALTING FISH

To preserve seafood, coastal residents frequently salt or brine their fall catches for use throughout the winter months. The fish are packed in large barrels and kept in unheated areas, such as barns, sheds, and basements.

Mitchell Morris of Smyrna prefers to salt spot. He packs his catch between layers of table salt in a barrel. The fish remain in the salt until twenty-four hours prior to use. Then Mitchell pulls the fish from the barrel and soaks them in fresh water to lessen the saltiness.

Bill and Eloise Pigott of Gloucester corn, or brine, their spot. They first eviscerate the fish, leaving on the scales. Next they place their catch in a light brine solution for several days. Then they drain and wash the fish and place them in a heavier brine solution. Like Mitchell, Bill and Eloise soak their catch prior to cooking. And Eloise cautions cooks not to remove the fish from the brine with a metal spatula; use wooden utensils.

Mitchell continues another coastal tradition—drying mullet roe. The best time for roe, says Mitchell, is in October when there is a full moon. He washes the roe, then covers the sacs in table salt. Later, he presses the roe between two clean, unpainted wooden boards in a sunny spot in an enclosed porch. The roe are allowed to dry for several days. Mitchell eats the sun-dried roe baked, fried, scrambled with eggs, or as is. "Old folks put roe in their pocket and eat it like candy," he says.

Even though many coastal residents still use these methods of preserving seafood, seafood specialists discourage their use unless you are experienced in the techniques, as improperly preserved fish could spoil. Experts recommend you freeze your catch instead.

MOLASSES GUNGER

2 cups plain flour
1 teaspoon baking powder
½ teaspoon salt
½ cup butter
½ cup sugar
1½ cups molasses
1 egg

Sift flour, baking powder, and salt. In a mixing bowl, cream butter and sugar. Add flour mixture to the butter and continue to beat. Add molasses and egg. Pour into a greased 8 × 8-inch baking pan. Bake at 350 degrees for 30 to 40 minutes or until a toothpick inserted comes out clean. Top with ice cream or whipped cream.

BILL AND ELOISE PIGOTT
Gloucester

Bill and Eloise Pigott cook Downeast-style. As natives of the true Downeast—the area between Beaufort and Cedar Island, so-called because sailing from Beaufort to Atlantic was downwind, or "downeast"—the Pigotts know the goodness of conch stew, the rewards of corned spot on a cold January day, and the sweet flavors found in a Downeast clam bake. And when cooking their favorites, Bill and Eloise often work together in the kitchen of their Gloucester home.

One of Bill's specialties is conch chowder, a Carteret County classic. There is even a saying that goes along with this dish: "If you ever eat conch chowder in Carteret County, you'll never want to leave." Bill says that cleaning and tenderizing this abundant mollusk is time-consuming, but, he adds, the results are worth the effort. He admits that the conch, which is more accurately a whelk, has a strong flavor for which many folks have to acquire a taste.

Eloise adds a touch of her own to Bill's simmering conch chowder—cornmeal dumplings. Holding true to Downeast tradition, Eloise finishes off every chowder, soup, stew, and mess of collards by rimming the pot with cornmeal dumplings. "We put dumplings in everything we boil," she says. "They used to say Carteret County cooks put dumplings in everything but the clothes they boiled."

By sharing the recipes she and Bill use in their kitchen, Eloise hopes to dispel some misconceptions about coastal cooking. "Tourists and people from outside the area think that all we know how to cook is fried fish, fried corn bread and fried potatoes," Eloise says. "That's a myth. Fried food is good, and some things are best fried. But we do know how to cook seafood other ways."

Eloise is as proud of the family's tie to this Downeast community as she is of her cooking. Around the turn of the century, Bill's father named the homes clustered along Core Sound "Gloucester" after the Massachusetts town of the same name.

CONCH CHOWDER

For easy removal of the whelk from the shell, Bill recommends freezing the mollusks first. Then thaw the whelks and the meat can be easily pulled out.

7 to 8 whelks, in the shell
1 quart water
1 to 2 thin slices salt pork
2 tablespoons butter
½ teaspoon salt
½ teaspoon pepper
2 to 3 Irish potatoes, diced
1 small onion, diced
1 teaspoon thyme
cornmeal dumplings (see recipe below)

Once the meat is extracted from the shell, keep only the cream-colored foot. Brush away the black coating with a stiff brush. To tenderize the meat, either pound or cook for 10 minutes in a pressure cooker.

After tenderizing, chop whelk into small pieces. In a large saucepan, add whelk, water, salt pork, and butter. Salt and pepper. Bring to a boil, reduce heat, and simmer 2 hours. Add potatoes, onions, and thyme 40 minutes prior to serving. Drop in cornmeal dumplings 15 minutes before serving. Serves 4 to 6.

CORNMEAL DUMPLINGS

2 cups cornmeal
1 teaspoon salt
½ to 1 cup water

In a mixing bowl, combine cornmeal and salt. Add just enough water to hold the mixture together.

Shape into small patties or cakes. Drop around the edge of chowder 15 minutes before serving.

DOWNEAST CLAM BAKE

Bill says clam bakes are favorite fare at church and community gatherings.

cheesecloth
1 fryer chicken, cut up
4 carrots
4 onions
4 medium Irish or sweet potatoes, whole
4 ears of corn, in the shucks
2 dozen cherrystone clams
kitchen string
water

In a large piece of cheesecloth, place 1 or 2 pieces of chicken, 1 carrot, 1 onion, 1 whole Irish or sweet potato, 1 ear of corn, and ½ dozen clams. Gather edges of cheesecloth together and tie with kitchen string to make a bag. Allow 1 bag per person. Pour two inches of water in the bottom of a 12-quart steamer. Place bags in steamer basket. Steam 1 hour. Additional water may be needed. Serves 4.

CLAM FRITTERS

2 cups clams, chopped
1 egg, beaten
½ teaspoon salt
¼ teaspoon pepper
½ to 1 cup plain flour
¾ cup vegetable oil

In a mixing bowl, combine clams, egg, salt, and pepper. Add just enough flour to hold mixture together. Drop by large spoonfuls into hot oil in a skillet. Panfry until golden on both sides. Serves 6 to 8.

CLAM HARVESTING METHODS

There is more than one way to get a hard clam out of its bed. North Carolina fishermen rake, tong, "sign," "swim," kick, and dredge clams from the estuarine bottom.

Traditionally most clammers, recreational and commercial, use either rakes or tongs to pry clams from their beds. Others "swim" for clams by crawling in shallow brackish waters. They feel for clams with their hands, knees, and feet. When a clam is found, the fisherman deposits it in a tub that sits in an inner tube. The tube and tub are pulled along by a rope attached to the clammer's leg.

Some clammers swear by the practice of "sign-ing" clams. At low tide, the mollusks make a keyhole impression in the sand while they are feeding. If a fisherman knows how to "read" the sand, he can quickly rake up a bushel or more of clams.

In recent years, North Carolina fishermen have begun mechanical clam harvest using hydraulic dredges and kickers. Hydraulic dredges dislodge clams from the mud using a nozzle and bring them to the surface with a conveyor system. The kicker uses a plate to deflect the prop wash from the rudder to the bottom, where it plows up clams. A heavy trawl or net is pulled behind the boat to capture the harvest.

Bill and Eloise say you must have plenty of time set aside for eating hard crab stew. Roll up your sleeves and get ready for the juices to run down your arms.

HARD CRAB STEW

16 to 20 live blue crabs
1 quart water
3 tablespoons crab boil seasoning
1 tablespoon vinegar

Place crabs in an 8-quart pot of boiling water. Add crab boil seasoning and vinegar. Cover and boil vigorously for 12 minutes. Drain crabs. Clean by removing top shell, snapping off mouth and eyes, washing away viscera, and pulling out grayish gill filaments. Break in half.

2 to 3 thin slices salt pork
3 quarts water
4 medium Irish potatoes, diced
2 medium onions, diced
2 teaspoons salt
1 teaspoon pepper
16 to 20 cleaned cooked crabs, halved (from above)
cornmeal dumplings (recipes, pp. 104, 116, and 138)

In a large pot, render fat from salt pork. Remove meat. Add water, potatoes, onions, salt, and pepper. Bring to a boil, reduce heat, and simmer until potatoes are tender. Place crabs on top. Rim pot with cornmeal dumplings and simmer 15 minutes longer. To serve, pile crabs on a platter and serve gravy and dumplings in bowls. Serves 4.

CRAB CAKES

1 pound cooked crab meat
1 cup Italian-seasoned bread crumbs
¼ cup mayonnaise or sour cream
½ teaspoon salt
¼ teaspoon black pepper
1 teaspoon Worcestershire sauce
1 teaspoon dry mustard
vegetable oil for deep-frying

Drain crab meat and squeeze out any remaining moisture. In a mixing bowl, thoroughly combine bread crumbs, mayonnaise or sour cream, salt, pepper, Worcestershire sauce, and dry mustard. Add crab meat and combine. Shape into patties or cakes. Fry in deep fat until golden brown. Serves 6 to 8.

PECAN PIE

1 cup dark corn syrup
3 eggs, slightly beaten
1 cup sugar
⅛ teaspoon salt
1 teaspoon vanilla
1 cup pecans, coarsely chopped
1 8-inch unbaked pie shell

In a mixing bowl, combine corn syrup, eggs, sugar, salt, and vanilla. Stir in ½ cup pecans. Pour into an unbaked pie shell. Bake at 400 degrees for 10 minutes. Reduce heat and bake at 350 degrees for 45 minutes. Five minutes prior to removing from oven, add remaining ½ cup of pecans to top of pie.

GEORGIE BELL NELSON
Harkers Island

For sixteen years, Georgie Bell Nelson dished up the noon meal for the kids at the Harkers Island Elementary School. While the school board dictated the menus, Georgie Bell admits that, every now and then, she would sneak in a little salt pork with the canned collards.

She retired from her post at the school a few years back, but she and her recipes are still cooking in the Nelson kitchen. The recipes, she says, are a combination of farm fare and coastal cooking. Even after fifty-some years on Harkers Island, Georgie Bell still calls herself a farm girl. But the farm she grew up on was right next to the water. When she got tired of working the land, Georgie Bell would pick up a bucket, head for the water's edge, and get a peck of clams.

After she moved to Harkers Island with her husband, Horace, Georgie Bell acquired a taste for some of the favorites of the natives. She remembers, for example, how the islanders got their reputation as loon-eaters. Although most people turned up their noses at the strong-flavored, fish-eating birds, Harkers Islanders parboiled loons outside over an open fire. Then they stuffed each bird with an Irish potato to help take away some of the "wildness" and baked them in the oven.

Another local favorite was pickled menhaden roe. She no longer remembers the recipe, but she says she will never forget the flavor. When menhaden with roe were being harvested, Horace traveled to the menhaden companies in Beaufort, where he was allowed to go on board the boats and strip the roe from the fish.

Today, it seems as though the large roe fish are less plentiful. And taking loons is illegal now. But as long as she can get fresh vegetables and seafood, Georgie Bell can dish up a feast for the table.

CLAM CHOWDER WITH CORNMEAL DUMPLINGS

2 to 3 thin slices salt pork
3 to 4 medium Irish potatoes, sliced
1 large onion, diced
1 quart shucked clams, chopped, and their juices
3 cups water
cornmeal dumplings (recipes, pp. 104, 116, and 138)

In a large saucepan, render fat from salt pork. Remove meat and combine diced potatoes, onions, clams, and water. Simmer over medium heat for 1½ to 2 hours. Drop dumplings in 45 minutes before chowder is done.

COLLARDS WITH CORNMEAL DUMPLINGS

5 pounds collards, washed and cleaned
½ pound salt pork, sliced
water
cornmeal dumplings (recipes, pp. 104, 116, and 138)

Place collards and salt pork in a large pot. Cover collards with water. Bring to a boil, reduce heat, and simmer for 1 hour. With a fork and knife, chop collard leaves while they are still in the pot. Add cornmeal dumplings and simmer 20 more minutes. Serves 8 to 10.

STEW-FRIED CORN

2 to 3 thin slices salt pork
6 ears corn
water

HARKERS ISLAND

Harkers Island used to be a community dependent upon the sea. Its people were fishermen and boatbuilders. Until 1941, the island was accessible only by boat. Before 1900, the only way to travel the thickly timbered island was along the shoreline at low tide and the only food was what could be grown on family plots or harvested from the surrounding waters. That isolation bred the independence and self-sufficiency that is still evident among the islanders today.

According to one Harkers Island native, "I used to think, 'I don't know what people eat that live in other places.' I says, 'What do they live on? They don't get oysters and clams.' The water was our living and the water was all of it. I thought you couldn't live unless you had seafood."

Besides a strong affinity for seafood, islanders also ate a variety of birds and waterfowl. They have been nicknamed the "loon-eaters" because they hunted and ate the loon, a bird which they stewed and flavored with rutabagas.

Just after the turn of the century, a path was cut across the island. Later that path was made into a road and paved. In 1938, ferry service began between Gloucester and Harkers Island. In 1941, despite a controversy, a bridge connected the island with Straits.

The days of isolation were gone. Outsiders began moving in, and the number of fishermen and boatbuilders dwindled.

In a skillet, render fat from salt pork. Remove meat. Cut corn from the cob. Then scrape cob with the dull side of a knife to get the remaining corn and juices. Add corn to the skillet and cover with water. Simmer over low heat for 20 to 30 minutes. Serves 4.

FRIED SWEET POTATOES

4 medium sweet potatoes, peeled and sliced
½ cup shortening or cooking oil

Panfry sweet potatoes in hot oil in a skillet over medium high heat until golden brown. Serves 4.

FIG PRESERVES

1 peck (8 quarts) figs
5 pounds sugar
lemon slices
sterilized pint jars

Place figs in a large pot and sprinkle sugar over top. Let sit overnight. Place pot on stove and simmer over low heat 3 to 3½ hours. Stir at the end of the cooking. Divide hot mixture into canning jars, leaving a ½-inch air space at the top. Add a slice of lemon to each jar for color. Seal jars and process 10 minutes in a boiling-water bath. Store in a cool place.

COCONUT PIE

5 slightly rounded tablespoons plain flour
⅔ cup sugar
¼ teaspoon salt
2 eggs, separated
1 cup evaporated milk
1 cup water
1 cup coconut
1 9-inch baked pie shell
3 tablespoons sugar

In a mixing bowl, combine flour, ⅔ cup sugar, and salt. Add egg yolks, evaporated milk, and water. Beat well. Pour mixture into a saucepan and cook over medium heat until it begins to thicken. Remove from heat and add coconut. Blend well. Pour into a 9-inch baked pie shell. Beat egg whites until the foam forms a soft peak. Slowly add 3 tablespoons sugar and continue to beat until whites form a stiff peak. Spread meringue over pie filling and bake at 350 degrees until meringue browns.

BREAD PUDDING

10 cold leftover biscuits
water
⅓ cup butter or margarine
⅓ cup shortening
1 teaspoon ground nutmeg
1 teaspoon cinnamon
½ cup evaporated milk
1½ cups sugar
2 eggs

Bread pudding is a favorite Downeast dessert. Georgie Bell uses leftover biscuits, and "the harder, the better," she says. Georgie Bell adds just enough water to dampen the biscuit crumbs.

In a mixing bowl, crumble the biscuits and dampen the crumbs with water. (No excess water should gather in the bottom of the bowl.) In a 9 × 12-inch baking dish, melt butter and shortening. Add crumbled biscuits to the dish and stir in remaining ingredients. Bake at 400 degrees until brown and crusty around the edges.

JESSIE SAVAGE
Morehead City

One way or another, Jessie Savage's career has always centered around good food. She got her first job in the kitchen by washing glasses. With the help of a friend—a chef—she learned to cook. From there, Jessie worked her way through the kitchens of Morehead City restaurants to a job as chef's cook.

Even when she took a break as a professional cook, feeding her four children kept Jessie in the kitchen much of the time. "I know the inside of a kitchen for sure, and I love to see other people enjoy food," says Jessie.

Now Jessie is a nutrition aide with the Carteret County Agricultural Extension Service. When she is not advising people about healthful eating habits, she is in her kitchen, making batches of hush puppy mix to send to her children who have moved inland or frying up her favorite—the hogfish.

The extension aide in her shows through when she chuckles at one cook's attempt to make corn-meal dumplings with fine-ground cornmeal. You can use yellow or white cornmeal, says Jessie, but never use anything but medium-ground meal for dump-lings. To emphasize her point, she pulls the proper selection from her pantry. "You can't make a good dumpling if you don't use the right meal," says Jessie.

Jessie says she has no patience when it comes to fishing, but she loves to cook the catch. Her favorite choices include hogfish, shad, and mullet. These days, fewer people know the goodness of these fish, laments Jessie. "People would rather buy a filleted fish."

Jessie says she couldn't cook without Worcestershire sauce. She uses it in almost all her recipes.

CONCH STEW

1 quart conch meat, frozen
4 cups water
2 to 3 slices salt pork
3 medium Irish potatoes, diced
1 large onion, diced
2 tablespoons flour
½ teaspoon thyme
2 tablespoons Worcestershire sauce
½ teaspoon black pepper
cornmeal dumplings (see recipe below)

Allow conch meat to thaw partially. Chop into small pieces. Place conch meat and water in a heavy pot. Cover pot and simmer over medium heat for 2½ to 3 hours. Additional water may be needed. In a skillet, fry salt pork until crisp and brown. Remove meat, chop, and set aside. Add potatoes, onions, flour, and thyme to the drippings. Sauté until potatoes and onions are almost done, but not brown. Add this mixture to the conch meat. Add Worcestershire sauce, pepper, and browned pork meat. Continue simmering until potatoes are done and flavors are blended. Add cornmeal dumplings the last 5 minutes. Serves 6 to 8.

Jessie cautions that adding too little water will make your dumplings heavy. And remember that she always uses medium-ground meal for her dumplings.

CORNMEAL DUMPLINGS

1 cup cornmeal
1 tablespoon plain flour
½ teaspoon salt
½ cup water

In a mixing bowl, combine dry ingredients. Add enough water to hold the mixture together. Pat dough in hands into small patties. Drop around the side of the pot of conch stew, chowder, or greens

CONCH

The conch in the famed Carteret County chowder is not really a conch at all. It is a whelk. Three types of whelk are abundant in Tar Heel waters: lightning, knobbed, and channeled. The conch has been pulled from Carolina waters since the days of the Indians, but there is some debate over whether the Indians ate the conch or merely used its shell as wampum, or money.

Clam fishermen, and especially clam gardeners, would like to see more whelks turned into chowder, since they are major predators of hard clams.

during the last 5 minutes of cooking. The dumplings will float to the top when done.

FRIED HOGFISH

Jessie says hogfish are sweeter than most fish. She picks around the bones and eats everything but the eyes.

3 pounds pan-dressed hogfish
½ cup cornmeal
1 teaspoon salt
½ teaspoon black pepper
½ cup vegetable oil or shortening

Dredge hogfish in cornmeal seasoned with salt and pepper. Panfry in hot oil in a skillet over medium high heat. Brown both sides. Serves 4.

SHAD ROE WITH SWEET POTATOES

4 shad roe
½ cup cornmeal

½ teaspoon salt
½ teaspoon black pepper
vegetable oil for deep frying
½ cup vegetable oil or shortening
  (for sweet potatoes)
2 large sweet potatoes, peeled and sliced

Dredge roe in cornmeal seasoned with salt and pepper. Deep fry until golden brown. Meanwhile, heat vegetable oil in a skillet. Panfry sweet potatoes over medium heat until browned on both sides. Serve roe and potatoes together. Serves 4.

SEA MULLET STEW

Jessie eats her sea mullet stew with a spoon.

2 to 3 thin slices salt pork
4 medium Irish potatoes, diced
2 medium onions, diced
water
½ teaspoon salt
¼ teaspoon black pepper
½ teaspoon thyme
2 teaspoons Worcestershire sauce
1 tablespoon plain flour
1 pod hot pepper
3 pounds sea mullet, pan-dressed
cornmeal dumplings (recipes, pp. 104, 116, and 138)

In a large saucepan, render fat from salt pork. Remove meat. Add potatoes and onions and cover with water. Boil potatoes until half done. Reduce heat to medium. Add salt, pepper, thyme, and Worcestershire. Sprinkle with flour to thicken gravy. Add hot pepper. Place fish in saucepan and simmer 30 more minutes. Add dumplings 5 minutes before stew is done. Serves 4.

CABBAGE

2 to 3 slices salt pork
½ large head of cabbage, sliced into thin strips
1 medium onion, sliced
½ bell pepper, diced
¼ cup water
1 tablespoon sugar
½ teaspoon black pepper

In a skillet, render fat from salt pork. Remove meat.
Add vegetables and water to grease. Simmer over
medium heat for 15 minutes. Sprinkle sugar and
pepper over vegetables and stir once. Serves 4.

Jessie says she likes her vegetables a little crunchy. Adjust your cooking time accordingly.

HUSH PUPPIES

2 cups cornmeal
¼ cup plain flour
½ teaspoon baking soda
1 heaping teaspoon baking powder
1 teaspoon salt
¼ cup sugar
1 cup milk
2 eggs, beaten
vegetable oil for deep frying

In a large mixing bowl, combine dry ingredients.
Add milk, then eggs. Let batter stand for 5 minutes.
Drop batter by the spoonful into hot deep fat in a
large saucepan and fry until golden brown.

Jessie uses whole milk instead of buttermilk in her hush puppy recipe because it is cheaper. When she wants to send some of the mix to her family, she substitutes powdered milk.

RITA GUTHRIE AND FLORA BELL PITTMAN
Salter Path

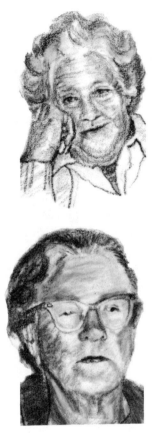

Around the first of September, the wind shifts and starts blowing out of the northeast. To natives, it is a sign that the mullet are about to run. To Rita Guthrie and Flora Bell Pittman, the northeasters signaled them to start the fire under their kettles; the men were about to start fishing and they were bound to be hungry.

Rita and Flora Bell cooked for a beach-seining crew from 1955 until 1963. Their day began with a 5 A.M. breakfast for twenty-five "big-eatin'" fishermen. Eggs, bacon, sausage, grits, and biscuits were the usual breakfast fare. But sometimes the fishermen would bring in a few fish fresh from the surf, and Rita and Flora Bell would add those to the morning menu.

As soon as the table was cleared and the breakfast plates cleaned, the women began the noon meal. And as soon as that meal had been gobbled down, they prepared supper. Rita and Flora Bell say they spent most of their days in the large kitchen.

Seafood was always available, and so they cooked a lot of it. But their menus never neglected fresh meats or home-grown vegetables. Each meal ended with a special dessert baked that morning.

BAKED BLUEFISH

3 thin slices salt pork
3 pounds bluefish, dressed with heads on
3 medium Irish potatoes, sliced
3 medium onions, sliced
1 tomato, sliced
½ cup water

3 tablespoons plain flour
½ teaspoon salt
½ teaspoon black pepper

In a skillet, render fat from salt pork. Transfer grease
to a baking pan. Lay fish in pan and add potatoes,
onions, and tomato. Add water. Sprinkle lightly with
flour and add salt and pepper. Bake for 45 minutes
at 350 degrees, basting the fish periodically.
Serves 4.

STEWED POMPANO

3 thin slices salt pork
3 pounds pompano, dressed with heads on
1½ cups water
3 sweet potatoes, peeled and sliced
3 tablespoons self-rising flour

In a large pot, render fat from salt pork. Remove
meat. Add fish and 1 cup water. Place sweet potatoes on top of fish. Sprinkle with flour. Add remaining water. Simmer over medium heat until fish flakes
and potatoes are soft. Serves 4.

SPARERIBS AND RUTABAGAS

4 to 5 pounds spareribs
2 medium rutabagas, peeled and sliced
water
2 teaspoons salt
1 teaspoon black pepper

Place spareribs and sliced rutabagas in a large roasting pan. Add water until ribs and rutabagas are
half-covered. Season with salt and pepper. Place in a
350-degree oven for about 1½ hours. Serves 4.

FRIED MULLET ROE

8 mullet roe
vegetable oil or shortening
3 tablespoons plain flour

Panfry roe in ½ inch of oil in a large skillet over medium low heat. Sprinkle with flour to keep the grease
from popping. Brown on both sides. Serves 4.

STEWED CHICKEN

1 hen, 3 to 4 pounds
water
1 teaspoon salt
cornmeal dumplings (recipes, pp. 104, 116, and 138)

Place hen in a stewing pot. Add water until it nearly
covers the hen. Salt. Bring to a boil, then reduce
heat and simmer until hen is tender. Add cornmeal dumplings and cook 30 minutes more. Place
chicken on a platter and serve dumplings separately.

MULLET AND WATERMELON

*Rita says mullet and
watermelon is a Salter
Path favorite. Serve the
fish with slices of watermelon and crunchy corn
bread patties.*

3 pounds dressed mullet
4 tablespoons salt
½ medium watermelon

Place mullet in a baking pan. Sprinkle with salt until
the fish are coated. Place in refrigerator for 2 hours.
Rinse away salt and allow fish to dry. Broil fish in the
oven until flaky. Serve with sliced watermelon.
Serves 4.

MULLET FISHERY

The mullet fishery began in North Carolina with the first settlers, and by the 1800s mullet was one of the main cash crops for the Outer Banks. During the fall mullet runs, Outer Banks fishermen built temporary camps made of small thatched huts near the beach. Lookouts kept watch on the waters for the dark mass that indicated a large school.

With one end of a seine net on the beach, part of the crew would row into the surf, positioning the other end of the net in front of the approaching fish. As the mullet filled the net, the boat slowly circled toward shore. After making the catch, the Bankers cleaned, salted and packed the mullet in barrels for shipment to inland markets.

Traditionally, the fishery was confined to beach seining operations. During its heyday people eagerly bought oceanfront property so they would have plenty of beach for pulling in the nets. But in recent years the beach fishery has dwindled. Cottages and condominiums limit beach access, and now most mullet fishermen gill net for the fish in the sounds and inlets.

The mullet, a fatty fish, is good baked, broiled, smoked, barbecued, and fried. Natives prefer to fry their mullet or barbecue them over an open fire. They eagerly await the full moon in October, when the largest roe mullet are said to be caught. The roe is eaten fried, baked, salted, or scrambled with eggs. Some even keep salted roe in their pockets for an occasional nibble.

SCALLOP FRITTERS

1 pound scallops, chopped
1 egg, beaten
1 small onion, chopped
1 teaspoon salt
½ teaspoon black pepper
4 tablespoons self-rising flour
shortening or vegetable oil

Place chopped scallops in a large mixing bowl. Stir in egg, onion, salt, and pepper. Add flour and blend well. Drop mixture by the spoonfuls into a skillet containing ½ inch of hot oil. Brown fritters on both sides. Serves 4.

LIGHTNING ROLLS

1 yeast cake
3 tablespoons warm water
5 cups plain flour
2 tablespoons sugar
1 teaspoon salt
⅓ to ½ cup lard or shortening
warm water

In a small mixing bowl, dissolve yeast cake in 3 tablespoons warm water. In another bowl, combine dry ingredients and add yeast mixture. Cut in lard or shortening. Using hands, work warm water into the mixture until dough forms a ball. Let dough rise in a warm place for two hours. Knead again until dough no longer sticks to hands. Pinch off dough for biscuits and roll in hands. Place on an ungreased baking sheet in a warm spot, cover with a cloth, and let rise again until double in size. Bake at 425 to 450 degrees until brown.

STOVETOP CORN BREAD

2 cups cornmeal
¾ cup self-rising flour
1 teaspoon sugar
1 teaspoon salt
cold water
¼ cup vegetable oil

In a large mixing bowl, combine cornmeal, flour, sugar, and salt. Add water until mixture is the consistency of pancake batter. Heat oil in an iron skillet. For patties, drop batter by the spoonful and panfry over medium high heat. For baked corn bread, pour batter into skillet and bake at 375 degrees until top browns. Serves 6.

RICE CUSTARD

1 cup rice, uncooked
2 cups water
4 eggs, beaten
3 tablespoons flour
1 5-ounce can evaporated milk
1 stick butter
1 teaspoon vanilla or lemon flavoring (optional)
1 tablespoon sugar

Rita and Flora Bell sometimes add prunes or raisins to rice custard. Rita advises boiling raisins for about five minutes before adding to the recipe to keep them from settling in the mixture.

In a large saucepan, bring rice and water to a boil. Reduce heat and simmer until rice is tender. To the cooked rice, add eggs, flour, milk, butter, and vanilla or lemon flavoring, if desired. Pour into a buttered 9 × 12-inch baking pan. Sprinkle sugar on top. Bake at 350 degrees until brown. Cool and slice to serve.

LETHA HENDERSON
Hubert

Letha Henderson was born and reared one mile from Swansboro on a farm called Roberson's Point on the White Oak River. Her family owned two large farms—one near Maysville, the other in Swansboro. They raised cotton, tobacco, peas, corn, and peanuts. Letha learned to cook by watching her mother, grandmothers, and occasionally her father. She tells this story: "I remember when I was a small child, and my mother was sick during a snow so my father cooked. He was a good cook. He killed some birds, cleaned them, and put them in a big iron frying pan with water. He put some sides of hog meat in with the birds. The meat had only been salted one or two days. We called it corned. Anyway, he made some dumplings and cooked the stew down to a slow gravy. We children thought it was the best stew we had ever eaten. My father called it 'blackbird stew.' You know, when children are hungry they can eat anything."

Once Letha had mastered the basics, she began cooking for the family while they were in the fields. She used iron pots and a wood stove. To cook on a wood stove, she first built a fire in the fire box. Once the heat had built up, she would "pull the damper and the heat would roll to the bottom of the baking barn." The baking barn is what we today call the oven.

The ingredients for her meals were of course "homegrown." The family had their own cow, chickens, hogs, vegetable garden, and orchard. They churned their own butter, took their corn to a nearby mill for grinding, and raised cane for molasses. Only the necessities that could not be grown in Onslow County soil—flour, coffee, rice, sugar, and black pepper—came from a store.

Naturally, Letha's family took advantage of the White Oak River and nearby brackish sound. Her husband and foster son ate a half-gallon of oysters every Sunday morning during the fall and winter. "The oysters were made up in fritters, using enough flour to hold them together and black pepper to taste," she says. "They were dropped in hot lard and fried brown. Um good."

Letha was no stranger to wild game. She knew how to cook up the likes of raccoons and bears. "I've cooked everything but snake," she says. "That's where I draw the line."

Letha's favorite time of the year came just after the first frost when the neighbors gathered for hog killings. Each family would bring its hogs for killing and the subsequent butchering. Families waited until after the onset of cold weather because the crisp air was needed to cool and firm the meat before butchering.

In carving up a hog, little went to waste. Usually carving was left to the men, but Letha proudly proclaims: "I have cut up a whole hog myself—no help. Only a sharp knife and hatchet," she says.

Fires roared and pots bubbled inside the house and out as the women rendered lard from the fat, cooked the livers and boiled the hogs' heads. Meanwhile, the men took the hams, shoulders, and bacon to the smokehouse to salt and sugar for smoking, Letha says.

LIVER PUDDING

1 hog's liver
2 medium onions, chopped
water
2 teaspoons salt
1 teaspoon black pepper
1 tablespoon sage

After removing the liver from the hog, check to see that it has no hard knots, says Letha. If it does, discard it. A hog liver should be soft like a leather glove, she says.

¼ cup cracklings (instructions, p. 16)
casings from small intestines of hog,
    cleaned and soaked overnight in salt water
    to make them tougher

Place liver and onions in a large saucepan and cover with water. Bring to boil, reduce heat, and simmer until liver is tender. Remove the liver and onions and put both through a meat grinder. Place in a mixing bowl and combine with salt, pepper, sage, and cracklings. Using a sausage stuffer, pack liver pudding into cleaned intestines, forming links. Tie off both ends. Store in refrigerator. Bake or panfry within one week.

SAUSAGE

Letha recommends frying a small portion of the sausage after it is mixed to test the seasonings. Correct if necessary.

6 pounds lean pork (use the trimmings from the
    hams, shoulders, or tenderloins)
4 pounds pork fat
3 teaspoons red pepper
2 tablespoons salt
2 tablespoons sage
casings from small intestines of hog,
    cleaned and soaked overnight in salt water
    to make them tougher

Put meat and fat through a meat grinder. Place in a large mixing bowl and combine with red pepper, salt, and sage. Using a sausage stuffer, place into cleaned intestines, forming links. Tie off both ends. Hang from the joists of a smokehouse or place in a smoker to dry. Cut off links as needed and panfry in a skillet.

PORK

As early as the eighteenth century, pork appeared on southern tables almost every day at practically every meal. It had replaced wild game as a major source of meat in the southern diet. Eighteenth-century author William Byrd said that pork was "the staple commodity of North Carolina and . . . with pitch and tar makes up the whole of their traffic. . . . These people live so much upon swine's flesh that it don't only incline them to the yaws, and consequently to the . . . [loss] of their noses, but makes them likewise extremely hoggish in their temperament, and many of them seem to grunt rather than speak in ordinary conversation."

But despite Byrd's unflattering remarks, hogs were animals that, properly butchered, cleaned, and prepared, could be literally eaten from head to tail. The head was made into souse; the brains scrambled with eggs; the feet pickled or boiled; the liver stewed into pudding; the intestines cleaned for chitterlings; the hams, shoulders, and bacon smoked; the lean trimmings ground for sausage; the fat rendered into lard; and the tails saved to flavor collards or greens.

The killing of hogs became a great social event in the South. When the days became cold, neighbors gathered to butcher hogs. The men usually carved the meat while the women made sausage and liver pudding and rendered the fat.

Letha says to put souse
in a glass loaf pan, not
a tin or aluminum pan.
She likes to place a slice
of souse on crackers or
corn bread and sprinkle
with vinegar.

SOUSE

1 hog's head, skinned, cleaned, and
    split in half (remove eyes, snout,
    and brains; leave jowls and ears)
water
1½ tablespoons black pepper
2 tablespoons sage
1 tablespoon salt

Place hog's head in a large pot. Cover with water and
bring to a boil. Reduce heat and simmer until meat
falls easily off the bone, about 3 hours. Remove head
from broth and cool slightly. Save broth. Remove
all meat from the bone. Put meat through a meat
grinder or chop finely. About ½ gallon of ground
meat should result. Skim as much grease as possible
from the top of the broth. Add black pepper, sage,
and salt to 1¼ quarts of broth. Add water if there is
not enough broth. Drop in ground or chopped meat;
mix thoroughly. The mixture should be the consistency of a thin pudding. Place in a glass loaf pan and
put in the refrigerator to congeal. Slice to serve.

Letha serves hog brains
and eggs with hot bis-
cuits for breakfast.

HOG BRAINS AND EGGS

brains from one hog
1 tablespoon bacon drippings
1 cup water
1 teaspoon salt
½ teaspoon black pepper
6 eggs, beaten

Wash brains in water. Remove all bone and veins. In
a skillet, place bacon drippings and brains. Add water, salt, and pepper. Simmer until most of the water
has evaporated. Separate brains with a fork. Brains
will be done when they change from a pink to a gray
color. Add eggs. Scramble. Serves 4.

STONE CRAB

North Carolina fishermen occasionally capture stone crabs in their crab pots. This species of crab has a range from North Carolina to Texas, but it is most abundant in southern Florida. Although they have a larger, thicker body than the blue crab, the most accessible meat is in their large black-tipped claws. Fishermen usually break off one of these claws and return the crab to the water, where it will regenerate the missing limb.

STONE CRAB CAKES

10 to 14 stone crab claws
1 egg, beaten
½ teaspoon salt
¼ teaspoon black pepper
¾ to 1 cup plain flour
1 cup vegetable oil

Steam claws 12 minutes in a steamer. Remove from heat and cool. Crack claws with a nutcracker or hammer and remove meat. Shred. There should be about 2 cups of claw meat. In a mixing bowl, combine crab meat, egg, salt, and pepper. Add enough flour to hold mixture together. Form into patties or cakes and panfry in hot oil until golden brown on both sides. Serves 6 to 8.

BOILED SHRIMP

2 cups water
1 pod red pepper

Letha remembers when shrimp were so plentiful that they hopped near the water's surface like falling rain. Her father

131

*would net the crusta-
ceans and "boil them
just like they came out
of the river with a pod
of red pepper and some
salt." The family headed
and peeled their shrimp
at the table, then dipped
them in a mixture of vin-
egar and black pepper
or melted butter. Along
with shrimp, "we had
corn bread, cucumber
pickles, and iced tea,"
she says.*

*Letha says she serves
coon hash with hot bis-
cuits or sweet potatoes.*

1 tablespoon salt
2 pounds shrimp, whole

In a large saucepan, bring water to a boil. Add red pepper pod, salt, and shrimp. Boil until shrimp turn pink, about 5 minutes. Drain. Serves 4.

COON HASH

1 raccoon, headed, gutted, and skinned
water
1 pod red pepper
1 teaspoon salt

Remove the scent glands from under the front legs and each thigh of the raccoon. Place raccoon in a large pot; add water, red pepper pod, and salt. Bring to a boil, reduce heat, and simmer until meat is tender. Remove from heat and cool. Pull meat from bone. Mince. Serves 4 to 6.

GRAPE PIE

1 quart scuppernong grapes
1 cup sugar
3 eggs, separated
1 cup cream
1 tablespoon cornstarch
1 9-inch unbaked pie shell
6 tablespoons sugar

Wash and pulp grapes. In a saucepan, simmer pulps over low heat until they form a thick sauce. In an-other saucepan, simmer hulls until tender. Remove hulls from heat and mash with fork or potato masher in a mixing bowl. Remove pulp from heat. Using a strainer, remove seeds from pulp.

In a mixing bowl, combine 1½ cups of pulp, 1½ cups of hulls, sugar, egg yolks, cream, and cornstarch. Mix. Pour into an unbaked pie shell. Bake at 300 degrees for 45 minutes or until the pie sets.

In another mixing bowl, beat egg whites and 6 tablespoons of sugar to make a stiff meringue. Smooth over the top of the pie, being sure to completely cover pie. Place back in oven until meringue browns.

Pie Crust

1 cup plain flour
¾ cup lard or shortening
3 to 4 tablespoons ice water

Letha likes her pie crusts short and flaky, and so she uses a lot of lard or shortening.

In a mixing bowl, cut lard or shortening into flour until it resembles cornmeal. Add enough ice water to hold the dough together. Roll dough with a rolling pin into a circle on a floured pastry cloth. Lay dough into an 8-inch pie pan and cut excess from edges.

APPLEJACKS OR PEACHJACKS

2 cups sliced apples or peaches, peeled
1 cup sugar
1 teaspoon cinnamon
½ teaspoon ground nutmeg
pie crust dough (see preceding recipe)
3 tablespoons vegetable oil or shortening

In a mixing bowl, combine apples or peaches, sugar, cinnamon, and nutmeg. Make dough, doubling the amounts from the preceding recipe. Pull off a small ball of dough. Place on a floured pastry cloth, and roll into a circle the size of a saucer. Place a heaping spoonful of fruit in center of dough. Fold dough over to form a semi-circle. Crimp edges to hold in fruit. Panfry in hot oil, browning on both sides. Makes 12.

Letha's mother served pound cake with persimmon beer. "My mother's father would get ripe persimmons, crush them, and put them on broom straw so the juice would run out into an enamel bucket," Letha says. *"It would be real clear like water. It never fermented, and the taste was different from any other drink."*

POUND CAKE

1 pound butter, room temperature
1 pound sugar (2½ cups)
10 large eggs, room temperature
1 pound plain flour (4 cups)
1 teaspoon lemon extract
1 teaspoon vanilla extract

In a mixing bowl, cream together butter and sugar until fluffy. Add eggs one at a time, beating after each addition. Add flour gradually. Stir in lemon and vanilla extract. Pour into a greased tube pan. Bake at 325 degrees for 1 hour and 20 minutes, or until an inserted toothpick comes out clean.

Letha says to cut young shoots from the yaupon tree when the sap is rising during the spring.

YAUPON TEA

15 to 20 shoots from yaupon tree
water
sugar to taste

Chop the shoots with a butcher knife or hatchet. (Be sure to discard any yaupon berries. They are poisonous.) In an iron pot over an outside fire, parch shoots until brown, stirring constantly. Or place on a cookie sheet and bake in a 350-degree oven until brown, shaking occasionally to brown all sides. Place in an airtight container until ready for use.

To make tea, crush shoots and use one rounded teaspoon per cup of water. Place in a large saucepan and add water. Boil 10 to 15 minutes. Strain. Add sugar and stir until dissolved. Serve hot or iced.

YAUPON

Yaupon tree roots were steeped to make a black tea that the Algonkian Indians used as a ceremonial purgative. But the early colonists found the leaves made a milder brew void of such nauseating effects. Yaupon tea has enjoyed extensive use by coastal residents since colonial days, and many drink it today.

SASSAFRAS TEA

Letha says sassafras tea is a good blood cleanser.

4 average-size roots from sassafras tree
1 gallon water
2 cups sugar

Wash roots thoroughly. Scrape if further cleanliness is desired. Place in a large pot with water; boil 15 to 20 minutes. Strain. Add sugar and stir until dissolved. Serve hot or iced.

FLONNIE HOOD &
DOROTHY HOOD MILLS
Burgaw

Flonnie Hood and daughter Dorothy Mills of Burgaw know that a meal is only as good as its ingredients. That is why they rely on vegetables fresh from the garden and fish or shellfish just pulled from coastal waters. For many years, their families have conspired to grow one of the biggest and prettiest gardens in Burgaw. They pick bushels of corn, beans, peas, tomatoes, potatoes, bell peppers, and more. And what they do not prepare fresh or share with family and neighbors, they preserve for the winter ahead.

Good food has always been central to their gatherings of family and friends. And the recipes that yield these much-demanded dishes are as treasured as any family heirloom. Flonnie passed along her favorite recipes to Dorothy, and now Dorothy is doing the same with her own daughters. The headings for the recipes in this third-generation "cookbook" tell a bit of family history: "Grandma Hood's corn bread" and "Mama's pound cake."

Dorothy often catches her own seafood. Whether in the sound or surf near her Topsail Beach summer home, she is always ready to cast a line, bait a trap, set a net, or man a rake. Almost as soon as she has her catch firmly in hand, she has it simmering in a stew, baking in the oven, or frying in a pan. And more often than not, there is a whole gathering of folks just waiting to dig a fork or dip a spoon into one of Dorothy's seafood dishes.

Flonnie and Dorothy respect such time-honored cooking traditions as fresh-baked biscuits, red-eye gravy, grits, and fried okra. They know these traditions will keep their family and friends pulling their chairs to the table for years to come.

CHICKEN AND PASTRY

Flonnie prefers to use a hen in this recipe because it has a better flavor than a fryer. And she occasionally tops her chicken and pastry with sliced boiled eggs.

1 large hen or fryer
1 to 1½ quarts water
1 to 1½ teaspoons salt
½ teaspoon black pepper
pastry (see recipe below)
2 hard-boiled eggs, sliced (optional)

Place chicken in a large pot and cover with water. Add salt and pepper. Bring to a boil, reduce heat, and simmer until chicken is tender, about 1 hour. Remove chicken and cool. Do not discard the broth. Remove all the bones, fat, and skin from the chicken. Tear chicken into bite-size pieces.

Return broth to stove and bring to a boil. Add pastry and boil 20 minutes. Add chicken about 5 minutes before the pastry is done. Top with sliced hard-boiled eggs before serving. Serves 6 to 8.

Pastry

Flonnie also adds a little pastry into fresh green peas.

2½ cups plain flour
½ teaspoon salt
⅔ cup cooled chicken broth

Combine flour and salt in a mixing bowl. Make a well in the flour. Add broth. Form dough into a ball, using a fork. Turn dough out onto a floured board and knead for five minutes. Using a well-floured, stocking-covered rolling pin, roll dough into a ⅛- to ¼-inch thick circle. Using a knife, make vertical slices every 1¼ inches. Cut horizontal slices every 3 inches. (Pastry should be 1¼ inches wide and 3 inches long.) Drop in boiling broth one by one. Simmer 20 minutes.

SQUIRREL AND DUMPLINGS

4 to 6 squirrels, skinned, dressed, and cut up
2 quarts water
dumplings (see recipe below)

Add squirrel and water in a large saucepan. Bring water to a boil, reduce heat, and simmer until meat is tender. Remove squirrel from broth. Do not discard broth. Pull meat from the bone and tear into bite-size pieces. Place the meat in simmering broth. Add dumplings and simmer 20 minutes longer. Serves 4.

Flonnie likes her dumplings soft. To achieve this texture, she rolls her dumpling mixture into a log and then slices off 1-inch sections and drops them into the broth.

Cornmeal Dumplings
⅔ cup fine-ground white cornmeal
⅓ cup plain flour
½ teaspoon salt
⅛ teaspoon black pepper
½ cup water or cooled squirrel broth

In a mixing bowl, combine meal, flour, salt, and pepper. Add water or broth. Roll the mixture into a 2-inch diameter log. Cut slices from the log and drop into the simmering broth. Simmer 20 minutes.

FRIED SQUIRREL

4 to 6 squirrels, skinned, dressed, and cut up
2 quarts water
⅔ cup plain flour
1 teaspoon salt
½ teaspoon black pepper
¾ cup vegetable oil

Place squirrel and water in a large saucepan. Bring water to a boil, reduce heat, and simmer until squirrel is tender. Remove squirrel from broth. Combine

CORNMEAL DUMPLINGS

If you want to stir up a controversy in coastal North Carolina, just ask a group of cooks how to make the "best" cornmeal dumplings.

First, you will have to define "best." For some cooks, it is a fat, fluffy dumpling. For others, it is thin and flat. Whatever the choice, coastal cooks often rim the pots of chowders, soups, stews, and collards with these two- to three-inch diameter meal circles.

Many coastal cooks use straight cornmeal to make their dumplings. Others stand by a mixture of one-half cornmeal, one-half plain flour. Still others work with a two to one, cornmeal to flour, combination. And those are just the variations in the base of the dumpling.

To the cornmeal, some cooks add water; others the broth of their soup, stew, or chowder. And the amount of water or broth varies according to the desired thickness of the dumplings. To finish off the dumplings, many cooks add salt and shortening, margarine, or butter; others, only salt.

Then there is the matter of shaping the dumplings. Some cooks pinch off bits of dough and shape the dumplings with their hands. Others take all of the dough, roll it into a log, and cut off one- to two-inch slices.

Finally come the variations in cooking time. Coastal cooks simmer their cornmeal dumplings anywhere from five to thirty minutes.

When all is said and simmered, there are about as many ways to concoct a cornmeal dumpling as there are kernels on an ear of corn.

flour, salt, and pepper. Dredge meat in flour mixture. Panfry in oil over medium high heat, browning each side. Serves 4.

PIG TAILS AND RICE

2 pounds pig tails, bite-size pieces
1 quart water
1 cup rice, uncooked

In a saucepan, add water and pig tails. Bring to a boil, reduce heat, and simmer until meat is tender. Add rice and simmer until rice is tender. Serves 6 to 8.

DEVILED CRABS

2 tablespoons chopped onion
3 tablespoons butter or margarine
2 tablespoons plain flour
¾ cup milk
1 egg, beaten
1 tablespoon chopped parsley
1 pound cooked crab meat
⅛ teaspoon black pepper
½ teaspoon dry mustard
1 teaspoon Worcestershire sauce
½ teaspoon sage
⅛ teaspoon cayenne
1 tablespoon lemon juice
6 to 8 cleaned crab shells, greased – Pastry Shells
1 tablespoon melted butter
¼ cup dry bread crumbs

In a skillet, sauté onion in butter until tender. Blend in flour. Add milk gradually. Simmer until thick, stirring constantly. Add egg, parsley, crab meat, pepper, dry mustard, Worcestershire sauce, sage, cayenne, and lemon juice. Place in cleaned, well-greased crab shells. Combine melted butter and crumbs. Sprinkle over top of each shell. Place shells on a cookie sheet. Bake in 350-degree oven for 20 to 25 minutes or until golden brown. Serves 6 to 8.

BAKED SHAD

1 3- to 4-pound shad, dressed
juice of 1 lemon
3 tablespoons butter, softened
1 teaspoon salt

Place shad on a large piece of heavy-duty aluminum foil or in a roaster with a tight lid. Pour lemon juice over shad and inside cavity. Rub fish with butter. Salt. Seal aluminum foil securely or fit lid over roaster. Bake for 8 hours at 300 degrees. Serves 4.

If you want to have baked shad for dinner, you should pop it into the oven just after breakfast, Dorothy says. It cooks all day, but when it's done, you can eat bones and all.

SHAD ROE AND EGGS

2 cups water
½ teaspoon salt
1 tablespoon vinegar
4 shad roe
vegetable oil or bacon drippings
6 eggs, beaten

In a saucepan, combine water, salt, and vinegar. Bring water to a slow boil and drop in roe. Simmer 12 minutes. Break the roe membrane while cooking to release the eggs. Drain water from roe. Grease a skillet with oil or bacon drippings. Add roe to beaten eggs and pour in a skillet over medium heat. Scramble with spatula. Serves 4.

Dorothy says her family anxiously waited for the shad to start running in the nearby Cape Fear River in February. The shad would run from February until April, and many mornings the family had shad roe and eggs.

RED-EYE GRAVY

drippings from a pan of fried country ham
½ to ¾ cup perked coffee

After frying country ham over medium high heat in a skillet, it will leave a crusty red residue and drippings. Remove ham and stir in perked coffee. Bring to boil and then remove from heat. Pour over grits or hot biscuits.

GRITS

Although Northerners scoff at this southern standby, Flonnie says there is a secret to good grits. The type of pot and water you use can make a big difference in the kind of grits you dish up, she says. Teflon-coated pans do not make good grits, and neither does water that is hard (contains abundant minerals). Flonnie's daughter, Florence Strickland of Raleigh, says she has "hauled water from Burgaw for years to cook my grits."

2 cups water
¾ cup grits (not instant)
1 teaspoon salt

In a saucepan, bring water to a boil. Add grits and salt. Reduce heat to low. Stir occasionally and add water as needed. Simmer 15 to 20 minutes. Serves 6.

RICE

Boiled rice is another southern breakfast favorite. Flonnie says she has cooked many a pot of rice for her family's breakfast.

1 cup rice
1 teaspoon salt
2 cups water

In a saucepan, add rice and salt to water. Bring to a boil. Reduce heat and simmer until rice is plump and fluffy. Serves 3.

CREAM-STYLE CORN

3 thin slices salt pork
4 to 6 ears fresh corn
1 cup water
½ teaspoon salt
¼ teaspoon black pepper
2 tablespoons plain flour
¼ cup cold water

In a saucepan, render the fat from salt pork. Remove meat. Using a knife, cut kernels of corn from cobs.

Scrape cobs again to remove pulp and juices. Add the kernels and scrapings to meat grease. Add 1 cup water, salt, and pepper. Bring to a boil, reduce heat, and simmer until corn is tender. In a jar, mix flour with cold water. Secure lid and shake jar until flour and water are thoroughly mixed. Pour into corn. Simmer an additional 3 to 4 minutes, stirring constantly. Serves 4.

BUTTER BEANS

2 to 3 thin slices salt pork
4 cups water
2 cups butter beans
2 teaspoons sugar

In a saucepan, add salt pork to water. Bring to boil, reduce heat, and simmer for 20 minutes. Remove meat. Add butter beans and sugar. Simmer 20 minutes. Serves 4.

Dorothy removes her butter beans from the stove as soon as they are done to retain their color and flavor. She says that butter beans cooked too long will become starchy. She prefers her butter beans soupy and serves them in a bowl.

FRIED OKRA

1½ pounds okra
½ cup cornmeal
½ cup plain flour
1 teaspoon salt
½ to 1 cup vegetable oil

Wash and cut okra into ¼-inch cross-sectional slices, discarding ends. In a mixing bowl, combine cornmeal, flour, and salt. Roll okra in cornmeal and flour mixture. Pour oil into skillet and place over medium high heat. Drop breaded okra into hot oil. Panfry. Turn with spatula to brown both sides. Serves 6.

BAKED CORN BREAD

1 cup yellow cornmeal
1 cup plain flour
½ teaspoon salt
½ teaspoon baking soda
1 teaspoon baking powder
2 tablespoons sugar
1 cup buttermilk
1 egg
5 tablespoons melted shortening
2 tablespoons butter or margarine, melted

Grease a 9 × 9-inch baking pan and place in a 425-degree oven to heat. In a mixing bowl, sift together cornmeal, flour, salt, baking soda, baking powder, and sugar. Add buttermilk, egg, and melted shortening and mix. If mixture appears dry, add more buttermilk one tablespoon at a time. Pour into hot pan. Pour melted butter or margarine over the top. Bake 20 minutes.

BISCUITS

Flonnie says she pulls off pieces of dough and pats it into biscuits. But Dorothy rolls her dough out to a ½-inch thickness on a well-floured pastry cloth and cuts the biscuits out with a can. But both agree that the biscuits should be put on the pan with their sides touching. This makes for softer biscuits, Flonnie says.

2 cups self-rising flour
½ cup shortening
½ to ⅔ cup buttermilk

In a mixing bowl, combine flour and shortening; blend with a fork to the consistency of cornmeal. Make a well; pour in buttermilk. Using hands, work the ingredients into dough. Either form dough into biscuits with hands or roll the dough out and cut with a biscuit cutter or glass. Place biscuits on a greased, floured pan, sides touching. Place in a 400-degree oven for 15 to 20 minutes until golden brown. Makes 6 large or 12 small biscuits.

PECAN PIE

3 tablespoons melted butter
1 cup sugar
½ cup white corn syrup
3 eggs, beaten
½ teaspoon salt
1 teaspoon vanilla
½ to 1 cup chopped pecans
1 9-inch unbaked pie shell

In a mixing bowl, combine butter, sugar, corn syrup, eggs, salt, and vanilla. Pour into a 9-inch unbaked pie shell. Sprinkle pecans on top. Bake at 375 degrees for 10 minutes. Reduce heat to 325 degrees and bake 25 minutes or until firm.

COLD-OVEN POUND CAKE

After pouring batter into the tube pan, Dorothy recommends bouncing the pan up and down on the counter to rid the batter of any air holes.

2 sticks butter, room temperature
½ cup shortening
3 cups sugar
5 eggs, room temperature
3 cups plain flour
⅔ cup milk
1 teaspoon vanilla
½ teaspoon almond extract
⅛ teaspoon mace
⅛ teaspoon salt

In a mixing bowl, cream butter, shortening, and sugar until light and fluffy (about 5 minutes). Add eggs one at a time, beating after each addition. Add flour alternately with milk, ending with flour. Add flavorings and salt. Pour batter into a greased, well-floured bundt or tube pan. Place pan in a cold oven and turn the oven to 350 degrees. Do not preheat. Bake 1 hour in a tube pan. Remove from oven and cool 5 minutes before removing from pan.

PERCY JENKINS & LORAINE JENKINS
Sneads Ferry

For over forty years, the Riverview Cafe in Sneads Ferry has been a family affair. Percy Jenkins and his brother-in-law operated the restaurant for thirty-eight years. Percy's brother-in-law sold the restaurant to him in 1969, and Percy continued to operate it until 1984 when he retired. Even then, he left four generations of the family still cooking in the kitchen. ´

Percy has been cooking all his life—first on a dredge boat, then in the army, in the restaurant, and at home. Percy's daughter, Loraine, says she learned by watching her father. By the time she was seven years old, she was working in the restaurant, standing on a Pepsi carton to reach the counter.

Percy and Loraine took pride in the Riverview's food. "We never threw everything into the same vat of hot oil," they say. Each day, there was a little something extra whipped up for their customers.

Percy's cooking has earned him a reputation in Sneads Ferry as an angel of mercy. He frequently takes jars of his oyster stew to the sick. Some claim the stew is a better remedy than medicine.

Percy dredges the shrimp twice before he fries them because he says that helps them retain more moisture.

FRIED SHRIMP

1 cup plain flour
1 cup cornmeal
1 teaspoon salt
½ teaspoon black pepper
2 pounds small shrimp, cleaned and deveined
¼ cup vegetable oil or shortening

In a mixing bowl, combine flour, cornmeal, salt, and pepper. Roll shrimp in the mixture and set on a platter for 20 to 30 minutes. Roll shrimp again. Panfry in hot oil in an iron skillet until golden brown. Serves 4.

FISH STEW

Percy and Loraine say this recipe is best with a flaky fish, such as flounder or drum. They like the stew served over rice.

2 to 3 slices salt pork or bacon
3 medium Irish potatoes, diced
½ teaspoon salt
½ teaspoon black pepper
water
3 pounds fish fillets, diced
2 onions, diced
1 bell pepper, diced

In a large pot, render fat from salt pork or bacon and remove meat. Put potatoes in pot, add salt and pepper, and cover with water. Bring to a boil and then reduce heat. Add a layer of fish, then onions and bell pepper, alternating to the top. Salt and pepper each layer. Bring to a boil, then reduce heat to low and simmer 1 to 1½ hours. (More water may be needed.) Do not stir. Serves 8 to 10.

CRAB SOUP

1 gallon dressed hard crabs
    (makes about 1 pound of crab meat)
1 onion, chopped
3 slices bacon
1 teaspoon salt
½ teaspoon black pepper
½ cup cornmeal
½ cup water

Place crabs, onion, bacon, salt, and pepper in a large pot. Cover with water and bring to a boil. Reduce heat and simmer 1 hour. Remove crabs and pick out meat. Add meat back into pot. Mix cornmeal with ½ cup of water in a jar, shake to mix, and stir into soup for thickening. Serve with crackling corn bread. Serves 4.

OYSTER STEW

In Sneads Ferry, folks say oyster stew is a "cure-all" for illnesses. "If you get so sick you can't eat oyster stew, you're really sick," says Loraine.

1 quart shucked oysters and juices
½ cup water
3 tablespoons butter or margarine
1 teaspoon salt
½ teaspoon black pepper
½ cup milk

Place oysters, their juices, water, butter, salt, and pepper in a large saucepan and bring to a boil. Boil until oysters begin to curl. Lower heat. Add milk, stirring continuously until stew is heated. Do not boil. Serve with hush puppies, saltine crackers, corn bread, or biscuits. Serves 8.

HUSH PUPPIES

Percy says you can add a small chopped onion in your hush puppies if you like the taste.

2 cups cornmeal
1 cup plain flour
1 tablespoon baking powder
½ teaspoon salt
1 cup water
vegetable oil for deep frying

In a mixing bowl, combine dry ingredients and stir in water. Let sit for 30 minutes to 1 hour. Drop mixture off spoon into hot deep fat. Fry until golden brown.

FRIED SCALLOPS

2 eggs, beaten
½ cup milk
2 pounds scallops
cracker meal
vegetable oil or shortening for deep frying

In a mixing bowl, combine eggs and milk. Dip scallops in egg and milk batter. Roll individually in cracker meal. Dip in batter again and roll in cracker meal. Drop scallops into hot deep fat and fry until golden brown. Serves 6.

FRIED SOFT-SHELL CRABS

Percy and Loraine use a mixture of cornmeal and flour on soft-shell crabs. Some say flour helps keep the crabs moist.

1 cup cornmeal
1 cup plain flour
1 teaspoon salt
½ teaspoon black pepper
8 soft-shell crabs, cleaned and dressed
½ cup shortening or vegetable oil

In a mixing bowl, combine cornmeal and flour. Salt and pepper crabs and dredge in cornmeal and flour mixture. Panfry in hot oil until brown on both sides. Serves 4.

BAKED FISH WITH CRAB MEAT

3 tablespoons vegetable oil
4 pounds fish fillets (bluefish, drum, flounder, or trout)
crab casserole (see recipe below)
2 to 3 pounds Irish potatoes, sliced
1 pound onions, sliced
½ teaspoon salt

¼ teaspoon black pepper
6 strips bacon

Lightly grease roasting pan with vegetable oil. Place fish two layers deep in the pan. Pack crab casserole around the outer edge of the pan. Layer potatoes and onions on top of fish, salting and peppering each layer. Lay strips of bacon across the top. Cover with foil. Bake at 400 degrees for 30 minutes. Lower heat to 350 and bake 30 minutes. Remove foil and bake 15 more minutes. Serves 12.

Crab Casserole
1½ pounds cooked crab meat
2 slices bread, toasted and crumbled
½ cup mayonnaise
1 egg, beaten

In a mixing bowl, combine ingredients. Add to baked fish.

Loraine says this stew will contain some bones, but it's worth picking around them.

STEWED MULLET WITH SWEET POTATOES AND CORNMEAL DUMPLINGS

2 to 3 slices salt pork
3 pounds mullet, dressed
1 small onion, diced
water
½ teaspoon salt
¼ teaspoon black pepper
2 sweet potatoes, peeled and thinly sliced
cornmeal dumplings (recipes, pp. 104, 116, and 138)

In a large saucepan, render fat from salt pork. Remove meat. Place fish and onion in the saucepan and add enough water to cover halfway. Salt and pepper. Bring to a boil, then lower heat. Place sliced sweet potatoes on top of fish and simmer over low

heat until fish flakes. Add cornmeal dumplings
15 minutes before stew is done. Serves 6.

BLUEBERRY DUMPLINGS

Biscuit Dough
4 cups plain flour
1 teaspoon baking soda
2 teaspoons baking powder
1¼ teaspoons salt
6 tablespoons shortening
1½ cups buttermilk

In a mixing bowl, combine dry ingredients. Cut in
shortening with a fork. Add buttermilk and work into
dough. Knead lightly. Pinch off biscuits. Roll each
biscuit in palm of hand and make a pocket for
berries.

Filling
2½ cups blueberries (or other similar fresh fruit)

Place a small handful of blueberries in the middle of
each piece of dough and fold dough over berries.
Pinch closed. Place on an ungreased baking sheet in
a 350-degree oven and brown until juices start seep-
ing out.

Sauce
3 eggs, separated
1 cup sugar
½ teaspoon cinnamon
¼ teaspoon ground nutmeg

In a mixing bowl, beat egg yolks and sugar. Add
spices. In a separate mixing bowl, beat egg whites
until stiff and fold into sauce. Pour sauce over dumplings and serve.

SUNSHYNE DAVIS &
JO ANN DAVIS GRIFFIN
Wilmington and Holden Beach

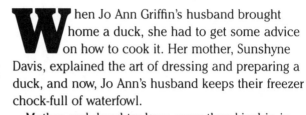

When Jo Ann Griffin's husband brought home a duck, she had to get some advice on how to cook it. Her mother, Sunshyne Davis, explained the art of dressing and preparing a duck, and now, Jo Ann's husband keeps their freezer chock-full of waterfowl.

Mother and daughter have more than kinship in common. Both married avid sportsmen and both know how to cook just about any wild game.

Sunshyne has lived in Wilmington for fifty years. Since she has been married, she has served such entrées as deer, bear, and frog legs. Jo Ann remembers that breakfast at the Davis home was not the usual bacon-and-eggs fare. "Mama would get up and fry venison and fix biscuits every morning before we went to school."

Eighteen years ago, Jo Ann moved with her husband James to Holden Beach. There, she continued the family tradition of cooking wild game and fresh seafood. She says living next to the water provides a constant source of food. "If we used more of what was available out there, we'd never have to go to the grocery store," she says. Her only rule about cooking seafood: "If we don't catch it, I don't mess with it."

DUCK AND WILD RICE CASSEROLE

2 wild ducks (about 4 pounds each), cleaned
3 stalks celery, julienned
1 onion, halved
1½ teaspoons salt
¼ teaspoon black pepper

water
1 7-ounce package long-grain and wild rice
½ cup chopped onion
½ cup melted butter
1 can sliced mushrooms
¼ cup plain flour
1½ cups half-and-half
1 teaspoon fresh parsley
½ cup slivered almonds

Combine first five ingredients in a large Dutch oven, cover with water, and bring to a boil. Reduce heat. Cover and simmer one hour. Remove ducks from stock. Strain stock and reserve. When ducks cool, remove meat from bones, cut into bite-size pieces, and set aside.

Cook rice. In a small skillet, sauté chopped onion in butter until tender. Drain mushrooms, reserving liquid. Add enough duck broth to mushroom liquid to make 1½ cups. In a saucepan, combine sautéed onions and broth and mushroom liquid. Add flour, stirring until smooth. Add mushrooms. Simmer over medium heat, stirring constantly until mixture is thick and bubbly. Add duck, rice, half-and-half, and parsley. Stir. Spoon into a greased 2-quart casserole. Sprinkle almonds over the top.

Cover and bake at 350 degrees for 15 to 20 minutes. Uncover and bake 5 to 10 minutes or until thoroughly heated.

SAUTÉED SHRIMP

Jo Ann says this is a messy, but delicious way to eat shrimp.

1 pound headed shrimp (not peeled)
1 medium onion, chopped
2 to 3 tablespoons prepared mustard

In a medium saucepan, combine shrimp, onions, and mustard. Simmer over low heat, turning shrimp frequently. Peel shrimp at the table. Serves 2.

STEAMED OYSTERS

Jo Ann and her husband steam oysters over an open fire outside. The oysters are done as soon as their shells slightly open. Then they are ready for the turn of an oyster knife and some melted butter, says Jo Ann.

24 oysters in the shell
melted butter

Place cement blocks on either side of an open fire. Cover blocks with a piece of tin. When the tin becomes hot, place oysters on top. Cover with a wet burlap bag. Steam until oysters begin to open. Serve with melted butter. Serves 2.

RED SNAPPER THROATS

Sunshyne says many people do not know about red snapper "throats," but they are some of the best eating around. The throats are cut from the breast of the fish in the shape of a "V." If you are purchasing snapper at the market, you can ask the fishmonger to reserve these pieces for you.

8 to 10 red snapper throats
½ cup lemon juice
¾ cup butter, melted
½ teaspoon salt
½ teaspoon black pepper

Place throats on a broiler pan. Brush with lemon juice and butter and sprinkle with salt and pepper. Broil until meat is white and flaky.

FISH CAKES

Sunshyne prefers to use grouper for her fish cakes, but she says any white meat fish will do.

1 pound fish fillets, cooked and flaked
1 medium onion, minced
3 eggs, beaten
1 cup bread crumbs
1 teaspoon salt
½ teaspoon black pepper
½ cup vegetable oil or shortening

In a mixing bowl, combine fish flakes, onion, eggs, bread crumbs, and seasonings. Mix well. Shape into patties. Panfry in hot oil over medium heat. Brown both sides. Serves 6 to 8.

PEA CRAB

You may find more inside an oyster shell than just the oyster. Many oysters serve as host for the tiny pea crab, or oyster crab. The small crabs take up residence as larvae. The females live permanently with their host, but the males are free-moving. At maturity, the females are pink, one inch in diameter, and soft-shelled. They neither hurt nor help their host, the oyster, but merely share its food.

Fishermen have long recognized the pea crab as a seafood delicacy. Many a fisherman will demonstrate his or her fondness for the tiny crabs by consuming them alive. Others eat the crab steamed along with their oysters or sautéed in butter.

VENISON STEW

2½- to 3-pound stewing chicken
water
1½ to 2 pounds venison
1 teaspoon salt
½ teaspoon black pepper
¾ teaspoon oregano
1 medium onion, quartered
4 cups chicken stock
4 Irish potatoes, diced
2 medium onions, diced
2 cups stewed tomatoes
1½ cups cooked rice

Place chicken in a large pot and cover with water. Stew over medium heat for 1½ hours. In another large pot, place venison, ½ teaspoon salt, ¼ teaspoon pepper, oregano, and quartered onion. Cover with water and stew 1½ hours. Remove chicken from pot and reserve 4 cups of the stock. Cut chicken into bite-size pieces. Remove venison from pot and cut into small chunks. Into a large pot, add chicken stock, potatoes, diced onions, tomatoes, rice, chicken, and venison. Season with remaining salt and pepper. Simmer for 1 hour. Serves 8.

VENISON MEAT LOAF

1 pound ground venison
1 pound ground pork
2 eggs, beaten
1¼ cups bread crumbs
1½ cups whole tomatoes, chopped
2 onions, chopped
½ tablespoon Worcestershire
1 teaspoon sage
½ teaspoon salt
¼ teaspoon black pepper
½ cup tomato sauce
1 bell pepper, sliced horizontally

In a large mixing bowl, combine meat, eggs, bread crumbs, tomatoes, onions, and seasonings. Blend well. Pat the mixture into an ungreased loaf pan. Top with tomato sauce and sliced bell peppers. Bake at 350 degrees for 1½ hours.

FROG LEGS

Sunshyne says to be prepared for the frog legs to jump in the pan. She covers her pan while she fries the legs.

1 pound frog legs
¾ cup plain flour
½ teaspoon salt
¼ teaspoon black pepper
½ cup vegetable oil or shortening

Skin frog legs. In a mixing bowl, combine flour, salt, and pepper. Dredge frog legs in flour mixture. Panfry in oil over medium heat until brown on both sides. Serves 2.

BEAR ROAST

Jo Ann says her mother fooled her with this recipe. After Sunshyne's children had eaten what they thought was her Sunday pot roast, she revealed that it was actually a bear roast.

2-pound bear roast
1 cup plain flour
¼ cup vegetable oil or shortening
2 10-ounce cans tomato soup
1 15-ounce can tomato sauce
2 medium onions, sliced
2 stalks celery, chopped
3 to 4 medium Irish potatoes, quartered
1 teaspoon salt
½ teaspoon black pepper
1 teaspoon seasoned salt

Dredge roast in flour. Pour oil into a large roasting pan and place over medium high heat on stove. Place meat in pan and brown on all sides. Add remaining ingredients, cover and place in a 325-degree oven. Bake until meat is well done and a large sharp fork can be easily inserted and withdrawn.

STUFFED TOMATOES

1½ cups shrimp (cooked, peeled, and chopped if large) or fresh tuna (cooked and chopped)
1 cup celery, diced
3 eggs, hard boiled and diced
1 medium onion, diced
juice of 1 lemon
½ cup cucumber, diced
1 teaspoon salt
2 tablespoons mayonnaise
6 tomatoes

In a large mixing bowl, combine all ingredients except tomatoes. Cut tomatoes into about 6 wedges each. Place in a baking dish and spread with fish mixture. Serves 6.

FRIED SWEET POTATOES

Sunshyne says fried sweet potatoes are excellent with fish.

vegetable oil for deep frying
4 sweet potatoes, peeled and sliced

In a large saucepan or deep-fat fryer, add 4 inches of oil and heat. Drop slices of sweet potato into deep fat. Fry until tender.

CHEESE-ONION BREAD

Jo Ann says cheese-onion bread is similar to spoonbread and has been a long-time family favorite at Thanksgiving.

1 cup cream-style corn
12-ounce package corn bread mix
1 cup sour cream
3 eggs, beaten
½ cup grated sharp cheddar cheese
2 medium onions, chopped and sautéed in butter

In a mixing bowl, combine corn, corn bread mix, sour cream, and eggs. Spread into a buttered casserole dish. Sprinkle cheese on top. Then add onions. Bake at 400 degrees for 40 minutes.

SWEET POTATO PIE

Sunshyne says sweet potatoes vary in sweetness, so you may need to adjust the amount of sugar you use. Just taste the pie filling before you put it in the pie shell. If it is not sweet enough, add more sugar.

6 medium sweet potatoes, boiled
1 cup milk
4 eggs, beaten
1 cup sugar
½ teaspoon vanilla
1 6-ounce can frozen orange juice, thawed

½ teaspoon cinnamon
½ teaspoon ground nutmeg
2 unbaked pie shells

Peel sweet potatoes and place in a large mixing
bowl. Mash potatoes with a potato masher. Add
milk, eggs, sugar, vanilla, orange juice, and spices.
Pour mixture into unbaked pie shells. Bake at 350
degrees until the filling is set and the crust is brown.

LEMON MERINGUE PIE

1¼ cups sugar
1½ cups boiling water
4 tablespoons cornstarch
juice of 4 small lemons
½ stick butter
3 egg yolks, beaten
3 egg whites
5 tablespoons sugar
1 9-inch baked pie shell

In a saucepan, combine sugar, water, and cornstarch. Bring mixture to a boil, reduce heat, and simmer until liquid is clear and thick. Add lemon juice,
butter, and beaten egg yolks. Simmer 5 minutes, stirring constantly. Pour mixture into the baked pie
shell. Cool before topping with meringue.

To make meringue, add 5 tablespoons sugar to
egg whites. Beat until stiff. Spread on the pie filling
and bake at 325 degrees until golden brown.

HALL WATTERS
Winnabow

For thirty-seven years, Hall Watters searched North Carolina waters for menhaden. He piloted the first spotter plane in the state, flying over coastal waters and pinpointing the dark masses of menhaden below. Once a large school of these fish was spotted, two small boats, called purse boats, embarked from a large mother ship to net as much of the school as possible. After the purse boat crews netted the fish, the mother ship would pull alongside and the catch was transferred to the larger ship's massive hold. By then, Hall often had spotted another school.

Hall got the job as a spotter pilot not only because he could fly but because he knew about fish. He grew up near the water at Kure Beach. "I didn't know it at the time, but I lived in the hospital that was there for the Civil War at Fort Fisher," he says. "My grandfather owned all that property, and we ate out of dishes that came off the blockade runner *Modern Greece*."

He learned a lot about fish from his grandfather, who fished for catfish using a trotline. He sold his catch, which ranged from two hundred to five hundred pounds of catfish a week, in nearby Wilmington for six cents a pound.

Since the family had no means of refrigerating the catfish, his grandfather kept them alive in a trap until the end of the week. "He had a trap that floated in the water," Hall says. "It looked like a submarine. It had a hatch on it and a sled front and bow. It had openings in it. Everyday when he worked his trotlines, he'd come in and throw his catfish in this trap. On Friday, he'd pull this thing up on the hill and take all the catfish out and skin them. On Saturday, he took them to market."

Hall's own fishing skills are more of the sporting

kind. Among his peers he is known as "the flying fisherman." Often he would spot schools of red drum or bluefish from his plane, land on the beach, and catch enough fish to feed his neighborhood. He holds three world records for channel bass, and in 1985 Hall's fishing knowledge earned him a spot on the N.C. Marine Fisheries Commission.

Hall treasures his knowledge of traditional cooking, which he often puts to use in his own kitchen. "A lot of traditional recipes just can't be improved on," he says. "It was simple, plain necessity cooking, but it was good."

FRIED CATFISH

2 pounds catfish fillets, skinned
½ cup lard or 3 thin slices salt pork
¾ cup plain flour
½ teaspoon salt
½ teaspoon black pepper

Cut catfish fillets into strips. In a skillet over medium high heat, melt lard or render fat from salt pork. If using salt pork, remove meat after frying. In a mixing bowl, combine flour, salt, and pepper. Dredge catfish strips in flour. Panfry in hot grease until golden brown on both sides. Serves 4.

STURGEON STEW

2 pounds sturgeon, skinned and chunked
4 medium Irish potatoes, peeled and diced
2 medium onions, chopped
2 quarts water
1 teaspoon salt
¼ teaspoon black pepper
2 tablespoons ham drippings

Place sturgeon, potatoes, and onions in a large saucepan. Add water. Season with salt, pepper, and ham drippings. Bring to a boil, reduce heat, and simmer for 1 hour. Serves 4.

BOILED POPEYE MULLET AND NEW POTATOES

After a big catch of popeye mullet, Hall's grandfather salted down his catch in large kegs for use throughout the winter. The fish were eviscerated, but not scaled or headed. They were salted once to draw out the blood, then rinsed and salted again in a watery brine ("enough salt to water to make a potato float"). One of Hall's grandfather's favorite breakfasts was boiled popeye mullet and new potatoes. "You eat the mullet right out of the skin," he says.

1 salted mullet per person
3 to 4 small new potatoes per person
water
salt
black pepper

Remove mullet from the brine 24 hours prior to cooking. Place in a large pot or pan of fresh water in the refrigerator. Soak 24 hours. Remove and rinse. Place mullet in a large saucepan; cover with water. Bring to a boil, reduce heat, and simmer. To test for doneness, slice away a small portion of skin and see if the meat flakes.

Meanwhile rinse potatoes and place in a large saucepan. Cover with water. Simmer until potatoes can be easily pierced.

When serving, crush the potatoes with a fork. Salt and pepper to taste. Serve mullet alongside.

EEL STEW

Hall says that eel has a sweet flavor. But he recommends eating any eel dish the day it is prepared because he says the meat will become "gummy" if it is stored.

2 pounds eel fillets, skinned
4 medium Irish potatoes, peeled and diced
2 medium onions, chopped
2 quarts water
1 teaspoon salt
¼ teaspoon black pepper
2 tablespoons bacon drippings

EEL

In America today, the eel is frequently shunned or ignored. But this snaky fish was a diner's delight among colonial settlers, and its fall from culinary esteem remains a puzzle even today.

For centuries another mystery about the eel created speculation. Where did eels come from? The inability to find roe or milt in eels led to twenty-three centuries of guesswork. Aristotle proclaimed that eels rose from the mud. Others said that eels were really horsehairs that had come to life. The British believed they originated from weeds.

The truth of the matter is no less fantastic. The eel swims hundreds of miles to the Sargasso Sea, a large section of the Atlantic Ocean southwest of Bermuda, to spawn its eggs. The tiny, transparent larvae are shaped like willow oak leaves. After they hatch, the larvae take a six- to twelve-month ride on the Gulf Stream and other currents, arriving in coastal waters from the Gulf of Mexico to Greenland. Many of them enter North Carolina's waters.

As they approach shore, the larvae undergo a metamorphosis, becoming rounded, transparent "glass eels."

Upon entering fresh coastal waters, the eels take on the pigment of the adults. Called elvers, the small fish measure three inches and are the thickness of a pencil lead.

These carnivorous young eels feed in fresh waters until they begin to mature six to thirteen years later. The yellow-green eel found in North Carolina waters reaches an average length of eight to sixteen inches. During the late fall, the mature eels turn a silver color and begin their migration back to the Sargasso Sea.

Cut eel fillets into sections. In a large saucepan, add eel, diced potatoes, and chopped onions to water. Season with salt, pepper, and bacon drippings. Bring to a boil, reduce heat, and simmer 45 minutes. Serves 4.

FRIED HARD CRABS

1 dozen hard blue crabs, alive
2 cups water

Hall says the only way to pull the meat from the shell of a fried hard crab is with your fingers. Be prepared for a messy, but tasty treat.

vegetable oil for deep frying
1½ cups flour
½ teaspoon salt
½ teaspoon black pepper
3 eggs, beaten

Drop live crabs in a 6- to 12-quart pot of boiling water. Boil 12 minutes. Remove crabs from pot and cool. Twist off claws and legs. Remove the crab's top shell. Scrape away the inedible spongy white gills and other viscera. Remove apron. Crack claws and extract meat.

Heat 5 to 6 inches of oil in a large saucepan or deep-fat fryer. Stuff claw meat into cavity of cleaned crabs. Season flour with salt and pepper. Roll the stuffed crabs in egg, then dredge in flour. Deep fry until golden brown. Serves 3.

FRIED MENHADEN ROE

Hall says menhaden roe is a delicacy that cannot be beaten. He eats fried menhaden roe like potato chips for snacks. Hall often freezes the roe on cookie sheets. Then he removes the roe from the cookie sheets for less cumbersome storage in freezer bags.

4 menhaden roe
vegetable oil for deep frying
½ cup flour
¼ teaspoon salt
½ teaspoon black pepper

Wash roe sacs, removing any remaining bits of intestine. Heat 3 to 4 inches of oil in a deep-fat fryer or large saucepan. In a mixing bowl, season flour with salt and pepper. Roll roe sacs in flour. Deep fry until golden brown. Serves 2 to 4.

MENHADEN ROE AND SCRAMBLED EGGS

Do not cook eggs with roe. The roe will not be done, Hall says.

4 menhaden roe
½ cup water

1 teaspoon vegetable oil
6 eggs, beaten

Wash roe sacs, removing any remaining bits of intestine. In a skillet, add roe sacs to water. Bring to boil. Break sacs as they cook to release eggs. More water may be needed as the roe cooks. Boil until roe eggs change from a grayish pink color to a yellowish brown color. Pour off any excess water.

Lightly grease another large skillet and warm over medium heat. Add broken roe to eggs and beat. Pour beaten eggs and roe into heated skillet. Scramble. Serves 3.

HICKORY NUT PIE

Hall remembers breaking open the hard-hulled hickory nuts against a steel block and then painstakingly picking out the meats.

1 cup light corn syrup
1 cup dark brown sugar
¼ teaspoon salt
⅓ cup melted butter
1 teaspoon vanilla
3 eggs, beaten
9-inch pie crust, unbaked
1 cup shelled hickory nuts

Preheat oven to 350 degrees. In a mixing bowl, combine all ingredients except hickory nuts and mix well. Pour into a 9-inch pie crust. Sprinkle hickory nuts over top. Bake 45 minutes or until pie sets.

E. L. LEWIS & "RED" OTIS RADFORD
Carolina Beach

E. L. Lewis and "Red" Otis Radford are partners in a seafood business; E. L. markets the shrimp and fish, and Red handles the crabs. In the kitchen of their little seafood market at Carolina Beach, the men divide chores according to their specialties. Red raves about E. L.'s stuffed flounder, and E. L. says his partner cooks the best catfish stew around.

For over ten years, the men have been cooking for each other and for customers who just happen to drop by at dinnertime. "Whatever comes off the boats that day, we might cook it," says E. L.

If clams happen to be the catch of the day, E. L. is glad to oblige his customers with a lesson in opening the mollusks. The best method, he says, begins with freezing the clams. He pulls a large chowder clam from the freezer, deftly inserts a knife, works it around the crack between the two shells, then gives the knife a quick twist. Scrape out the grit around the clam's mouth, says E. L., "but be sure to save all the juice that you can."

E. L. and Red say cooking—especially seafood—just comes naturally to them because they have lived near the water for so long. Red, originally from Goldsboro, moved to Carolina Beach in 1958. "I just turned out to be a fisherman," he says. E. L. is from Boone's Neck in Brunswick County, where, he says, he was born "with an oyster knife in one hand and a piece of bread in the other."

CLAM CHOWDER

4 Irish potatoes, diced
1 large onion, diced
water
2 dozen chowder clams, chopped, and their juices
1 teaspoon black pepper

In a large saucepan, cover potatoes and onions with water and bring to a boil. Reduce heat and simmer for 20 minutes. Add clams and their juices to the saucepan. Boil for 3 minutes. (For thicker chowder, add water mixed with regular cornmeal before final 3 minutes.) Add pepper. Makes about 4 quarts.

STUFFED FLOUNDER

1 3- to 4-pound flounder, whole
crab dressing (see recipe below)

Eviscerate flounder, leaving on the head and tail. Cut out mouth and eyes. With a knife, make diagonal gashes across the body about 2 inches apart. Slide knife under each gash, separating flesh from bones. Stuff crab dressing under gashes and into mouth cavity. Bake in a greased pan at 350 degrees for 1 hour or until fish flakes. Baste fish as it cooks in its own juices. Serves 6 to 8.

Crab Dressing
4 medium Irish potatoes, peeled
water
1 medium to large onion, diced
¼ cup vegetable oil or shortening
corn bread (see recipe below), crumbled
1 pound cooked crab meat

In a saucepan, boil potatoes in water until tender. Dice as for potato salad. In a small skillet, lightly sauté onions in oil. In a large skillet, combine potatoes, onions, crumbled corn bread, and crab meat. Sauté over medium heat for about 10 minutes.

Corn Bread
⅔ cup plain flour
1⅓ cups cornmeal
1 teaspoon salt
1 cup water
½ cup vegetable oil

In a mixing bowl, combine flour, cornmeal, and salt with water. (It should have the consistency of pancake batter.) Pour oil into skillet and place over medium heat. Spoon batter into skillet, making cakes. Fry on both sides and set aside to cool.

CLAM FRITTERS

2 dozen chowder clams and their juices
1 medium onion, diced
⅔ cup plain flour
½ cup cornmeal
½ teaspoon black pepper
¼ cup vegetable oil or shortening

Chop clams. In a mixing bowl, combine clams, their juices, and onion. In a separate bowl, combine flour, cornmeal, and pepper. Slowly add dry ingredients to the chopped clams, stopping while mixture is still moist enough to form patties. (You may not need all the flour and cornmeal mixture.) Panfry patties in hot oil over medium heat until brown on both sides. Serves 6 to 8.

CHOWDER

Mention the word "chowder" and three things come to mind—New England, seafood, and potatoes. Chowders are not limited to the Northeast, however. Other parts of the country quickly learned about the filling nature of a slow-cooked, hearty chowder, and coastal North Carolina is no exception. Cooks make chowders from clams, whelks, and a variety of saltwater fish.

Basically, there are two traditional methods for cooking a chowder. In one method, the cook layers slices of fish and vegetables into a sauce-pan or baking dish, covers them with liquid, and bakes or simmers the chowder over low heat. In the other method, the cook cuts the fish and vegetables into chunks, covers them with liquid, stirs them together, and cooks slowly.

Coastal Carolina cooks use both methods. They also tend to flavor their chowders with the traditional ingredients of salt pork and onions. When making clam chowder, North Carolinians, unlike New Englanders or Manhattaners, add only water to the pot.

CATFISH STEW

½ pound salt pork, diced
4 pounds catfish (skinned, filleted, and cut into pieces)
4 pounds Irish potatoes, sliced
2 medium onions, sliced
1 teaspoon salt
½ teaspoon pepper
water

For a different flavor, Red sometimes pours a 12-ounce can of tomato paste over the stew and adds a layer of sliced boiled eggs about 30 minutes before the stew is done.

Place diced salt pork in a Dutch oven. Add a layer of catfish, then potatoes, then onions. Continue layering ingredients to the top. Sprinkle salt and pepper on top. Add water to within ½ inch of the top layer. Cover and bake at 300 degrees for 3 hours. Serves 8.

CRAB CAKES

1 pound cooked crab meat
2 eggs, beaten
½ pound onions, chopped
½ cup cornmeal
½ cup flour
1 teaspoon salt
½ teaspoon black pepper
¼ cup vegetable oil or shortening

In a large mixing bowl, combine crab, eggs, and onions. In a separate bowl, combine cornmeal, flour, salt, and pepper. Add just enough of the cornmeal mixture to hold crab meat together when patties are formed. Panfry patties in hot oil, browning each side. Serves 6 to 8.

REFERENCES

Coastwatch. UNC Sea Grant College Program, Raleigh, N.C.

McClane, A. J., *The Encyclopedia of Fish Cookery*. Holt, Rinehart and Winston, New York. 1977.

Taylor, Joe Gray. *Eating, Drinking and Visiting in the South: An Informal History*. Louisiana State University Press, Baton Rouge. 1982.

INDEX

Misc.
Watermelon rind pickles 7
Pickled Figs 14
Cucumber relish 19
Spiced peaches 24
Jerusalem artichoke pickles 43
Fig preserves 112
Red eye gravy 141

Breads
Baking P. yeast biscuits 18
Corn pone bread 74
Corn meal Dumplings 116
Corn Bread Patties 125
Buttermilk corn bread 144
✓ Cheese - onion Bread 158

Vegetables
Fried Sweet Potatoes 12
Fried Rutabaga patties 12
Corn Pudding 23
Crookneck fried Squash 31
Fried Squash Patties - 31
Rutabagas - salt Pork 49
Mashed Turnips 49
green beans, ham, Potatoes 50
Rutabagas - Salt pork 97
✓ Cabbage Salt Pork, b. rum 119
Butter beans + Pork 143
Fried Okra 143

Salads
Crab 28
Tuna - egg 55
✗ Cole Slaw - Pickle relish

Seafood

Crab Casserole P. 11, 93
Fried Scallops P 91, 124
Down-East Clam Bake 105
Clam Fritters 105
vv Crab Cakes 107, 170 with cornmeal
Deviled Crab in Pastry Shells 140
vv Sautéed Shrimp + onion + mustard 153
vv Shrimp stuffed tomatoes P. 157
Clam Fritters 168

Other Meats

Spare ribs - Rutabagas 121
Home made Sausage 128
Chicken - noodles +
   hand b. eggs P. 137
Ham + Red eye gravy
            141

Dessert)
Cherry cobbler 26
Custard raisin pie 33
Lemon chess pie 44
* Chocolate Pound cake 52
* Pineapple upside down cal
Chilled Layered Blueberry d.
xxx Brown Sugar cake 70
Pecan Pie 108
Bread Pudding with
      Biscuits   — 11
Baked Rice Pudding 12
Fried apple Turnovers 1
Pound cake with
   almond extract
      + mace 145